Quality vs. Quantity

Is There A Middle Way?

T.D. Errol

Quality verses Quantity: Is There a Middle Way?

Quality vs. Quantity:
Is There a Middle Way?

T.D. Errol

Quality versus Quantity: Is There a Middle Way?
By T.D. Errol

Copyright © 2024 by T.D. Errol
All rights reserved. No part of this book may be reproduced or transmitted in any form or by any means, electronic or mechanical, including photocopying, recording, or any information storage and retrieval system, without the publisher's prior written permission, except where permitted by law.

Published by Errol Publishing

This is a work of nonfiction. Names, characters, businesses, places, events, and incidents are either the products of the author's imagination or used in a fictitious manner. Any resemblance to actual persons, living or dead, or events is coincidental.

Cover Design by Clifford Daiss
Edited by Clifford Daiss

First Edition: September 2024
ISBN: 9798340564436
Imprint: Independently published

Printed in the United States of America

Disclaimer

The information in this book is provided with the understanding that the author and publisher are not rendering professional advice or services to the individual reader. The contents of this book are for informational purposes only and should not be used as a substitute for professional advice.

Dedication

To Anne,
You are my guiding star, the constant light that brightens my path. Your unwavering support and love are the threads that weave the fabric of my life. This journey, like all the others, is for you. May we continue to create and cherish moments of joy, laughter, and discovery together.

About the Author

T.D. Errol passionately advocates personal growth, quality management, and productivity. With a career spanning over 40 years, T.D. has explored diverse fields, including process improvement, project management, personal development, and business strategy. As the author of multiple books, such as *The Kanban Life* and *Time Block Like a Pro!*, T.D. offers practical guidance on achieving balance, efficiency, and continuous improvement.

T.D. is driven to help individuals and organizations thrive, combining a wealth of experience with a passion for excellence. Known for insightful analysis, engaging narratives, and actionable advice, his writing resonates with readers seeking meaningful change. T.D. enjoys reading and taking strolls when not writing, always observing how businesses operate to inspire new ideas.

Believing that growth is a journey, not a destination, T.D. inspires others through his books to pursue quality and fulfillment in all aspects of life.

Quality verses Quantity: Is There a Middle Way?

Forward

In our fast-paced, results-driven world, we are constantly faced with choices. Often, we are led to believe that these choices lie at two opposing extremes: quantity or quality. As consumers, business leaders, and individuals, we are conditioned to prioritize one. Yet, as I reflect on the experiences of successful industries, meaningful personal achievements, and sustainable growth, I am reminded of an ancient concept that offers a profound insight into this dilemma: the idea of Yin and Yang.

Yin and Yang represent dualities that are not merely opposites but interconnected and interdependent forces. Much like these symbols of balance, quality, and quantity are not mutually exclusive. They are two sides of the same coin, each playing a vital role in the overall picture. Without quantity, our efforts lack the reach to create impact; without quality, those efforts risk becoming hollow and devoid of value or substance.

This book explores the delicate dance between these two forces. By examining historical trends, business strategies, and personal philosophies, it seeks to uncover the middle way. Quality and quantity coexist harmoniously on this path, reinforcing each other and creating lasting value.

In a world that often prioritizes more, better, or perfect over plentiful, this book reminds us that true success lies in the balance. Just as Yin cannot thrive without Yang, and day cannot exist without night, we cannot achieve sustainable growth or fulfillment by focusing solely on one end of the spectrum.

I invite you to explore the pages ahead with an open mind, considering how you might apply these principles to your professional endeavors and personal life. The journey toward finding a balance between quality and quantity is a nuanced one. Through this exploration, I hope you will

Quality verses Quantity: Is There a Middle Way?
discover the tools and insights to navigate it with wisdom and intentionality.

Quality verses Quantity: Is There a Middle Way?

Contents

Introduction	11
The Origins of the Debate	15
Quality and Quantity in Manufacturing	19
High-Quality Products vs. Market Share	27
Quality and Quantity in Retail	39
Quality vs. Quantity in Product Development	45
Quality and Quantity in Personal Development and Lifestyle Choices	53
The Middle Way	69
Challenges and Opportunities	93
Case Studies and Personal Stories	119
Future Trends and Innovations	141
Reflecting on the Journey	165
Appendix	179

Quality verses Quantity: Is There a Middle Way?

Quality verses Quantity: Is There a Middle Way?

Introduction

The Timeless Tug-of-War: Quality vs. Quantity

Picture a bustling marketplace, alive with energy. On one side, vendors display endless rows of goods, eager for customers to make a selection. On the other hand, artisans exhibit their meticulously crafted wares, each a testament to skill and dedication. This scene encapsulates an ancient debate: the tension between quality and quantity.

Throughout history, this debate has shaped decisions, industries, and the lives of many. Balancing these two forces has driven human progress from the mass production marvels of the Industrial Revolution to the handcrafted elegance of bespoke artisans. Far from being an abstract concept, this dichotomy informs our everyday choices—whether in the products we buy or how we spend our time and resources.

Historical Context and Evolution

The roots of this debate run deep in ancient philosophy. Aristotle's doctrine of the "Golden Mean" called for balance, advocating that virtue lies between deficiency and excess. Similarly, Confucian ideals of harmony and moderation reflect the quest to strike a balance between quality and quantity.

In ancient Rome, the concept of *quality* was closely tied to craftsmanship and excellence. Artisans were revered for their meticulous attention to detail and valued for the inherent quality of their work. This reverence persisted into the Middle Ages, when guilds enforced strict standards of superiority in their trades.

The Industrial Revolution, however, marked a shift towards quantity. Factories produced goods at unprecedented rates, driving economies forward. Mass production became synonymous with progress, and efficiency took precedence over all else. Yet even in this age of mass production, pioneers like W. Edwards Deming championed the importance of quality, introducing concepts of quality control that balanced efficiency with excellence.

Why This Book?

In our fast-paced, modern world, the debate between quality and quantity is more urgent than ever. Businesses struggle to maintain standards while scaling up. Educators balance the depth of knowledge with the breadth of curricula. On a personal level, we all seek meaning amidst the pressures of consumerism and the demands of productivity.

This book examines the dynamics of manufacturing, education, business, retail, and personal development, offering strategies, insights, and real-world examples for achieving balance. Through thoughtful analysis and compelling stories, it asks: Can high standards coexist with high output? How do businesses sustain growth without compromising quality? What can we learn from educational systems that manage both depth and breadth? And how can individuals strike a harmony between personal and professional demands?

The Journey Ahead

As we embark on this journey, we'll learn from those who have navigated this delicate balance. From high-end manufacturers to innovative educators, each chapter offers lessons and practical applications that are both informative and engaging. We'll explore principles like Lean production, which aims to produce more and better. We'll examine education systems that favor deep learning over superficial knowledge and businesses that prioritize quality even in competitive markets.

But this book is more than just case studies and theories—it's an invitation to rethink how we approach our world. It challenges us to question the status quo, seek balance, and find a middle way that harmonizes quality with quantity.

A Promise of Insight and Engagement

This book promises an engaging exploration of one of today's most pressing issues. Whether you're a business leader, educator, craftsman,

Quality verses Quantity: Is There a Middle Way?

or someone seeking balance in your personal life, the insights shared here will resonate. You will encounter timeless philosophies, modern innovations, and practical experiences as you turn the pages of this book.

Welcome to "Quality versus Quantity: Is There a Middle Way?" Let us explore how finding balance can lead to a more harmonious and fulfilling life together.

Quality verses Quantity: Is There a Middle Way?

The Origins of the Debate

Historical Examples and Philosophical Perspectives

The tension between quality and quantity is an age-old debate deeply rooted in both philosophical and practical contexts. Examining historical examples and ancient philosophies reveals how this dichotomy has shaped our thinking, work, and production.

Aristotle's Golden Mean
Aristotle's Doctrine of the Golden Mean offers a timeless perspective on balance. For Aristotle, virtue lies between deficiency and excess; courage, for example, exists between recklessness and cowardice. This middle ground applies to personal ethics and broader debates about quality and quantity.
In terms of productivity, Aristotle's philosophy suggests that neither an overwhelming focus on quantity nor an exclusive pursuit of quality leads to success. An employee who produces numerous reports without depth or takes too long to achieve perfection misses the balance that true virtue requires. The Golden Mean encourages a harmonious integration of both. In education, it suggests a curriculum that provides breadth while allowing enough depth for meaningful learning. The same logic applies to personal endeavors, such as fitness or work-life balance—success is found through moderation and sustainability.

Confucius and Harmony
Confucius' concept of harmony also speaks to the quality versus quantity debate. He advocated for balance and moderation in personal conduct, governance, and education. Confucius believed that a well-ordered society functions like a finely tuned instrument, with all parts working harmoniously. In governance, for instance, policies should strike a balance between the ethical production of goods and economic growth. In personal life, a balanced approach to success avoids the

extremes of burnout and underachievement, fostering a well-rounded and harmonious existence.

Roman and Medieval Views on Quality

The Romans, emphasizing *Qualitas*, were masters of craftsmanship and excellence. Roman engineering marvels, such as aqueducts and roads—especially the Via Appia and the Pantheon—symbolize their commitment to lasting quality. This pursuit of excellence influenced how societies understood the value of building for the long term, a principle equally crucial in today's debates on sustainability and enduring craftsmanship.

During the medieval period, guilds played a crucial role in maintaining high-quality standards in various trades. By regulating who could practice a trade, enforcing strict standards, and offering apprenticeships, guilds ensured that only well-trained individuals produced goods, thereby fostering economic stability and trust. This model underscores the importance of rigorous quality control, which remains a key aspect of modern production practices.

Enlightenment and Industrial Revolution Perspectives

The Enlightenment: Rationalism and Excellence

Enlightenment philosophers such as John Locke and Emmanuel Kant made significant contributions to our understanding of quality. Locke's empiricism emphasized the importance of gaining knowledge through sensory experience and rational thought, a foundation for modern educational systems that value depth and understanding over the mere accumulation of facts. Kant's concept of moral duty emphasized pursuing excellence, highlighting that the best outcomes are driven by principles rather than quantity alone.

The Industrial Revolution: The Triumph of Quantity

The Industrial Revolution, epitomized by innovations such as Henry Ford's assembly line, revolutionized production by focusing on efficiency and increased output. Mass production enabled the democratization of goods, making products more accessible to a broader audience. However, this shift often came at the cost of quality. The era marked a clear transition, where the emphasis on quantity sometimes led to a decrease in attention to craftsmanship and durability, revealing the dangers of prioritizing output over excellence.

Key Thinkers and Their Views

Frederick Winslow Taylor: Scientific Management

Taylor's principles of scientific management sought to enhance productivity by breaking down tasks into smaller components and standardizing processes. While his methods improved efficiency, they often reduced work to monotonous tasks, leading to critiques about dehumanizing labor. His emphasis on standardization provided consistency but sometimes at the expense of creativity and worker satisfaction.

W. Edwards Deming: Quality Control and Continuous Improvement

Deming, a key figure in modern quality management, argued that quality should be an integral part of every process. His philosophy of continuous improvement—embodied in his Plan-Do-Check-Act cycle—emphasized that true success comes from constant refinement and systemic thinking. Deming's ideas, adopted enthusiastically in post-war Japan, laid the foundation for Total Quality Management (TQM), which focused on quality at every production level.

Philosophical Reflections and Ethical Considerations

Modern Thinkers: Robert Pirsig and Michael Sandel

In his book *Zen and the Art of Motorcycle Maintenance*, Robert Pirsig explores quality as an experiential concept that transcends the classical versus romantic dichotomy in understanding the world. Pirsig's narrative emphasizes the value of craftsmanship and mindfulness, advocating for an approach to work and life that values depth over volume.

Philosopher Michael Sandel critiques the commodification of modern life, arguing that when market values infiltrate areas traditionally valued for their intrinsic worth, such as education and healthcare, the focus on quantity undermines the quality of those experiences. Both thinkers urge us to consider what is lost when quantity eclipses quality in our pursuit of success.

Ethical Considerations: Balancing Quality, Worker Welfare, and Environmental Sustainability

The modern debate on quality versus quantity extends into the realm of ethics, particularly in its impact on workers, consumers, and the environment. A relentless focus on output can lead to poor working conditions and exploitative labor practices while producing cheap, short-lived goods increases environmental degradation. Ethical business practices, then, must find a balance between high-quality production and responsible, sustainable growth.

Relevance to Modern Context

Lessons from history and philosophy provide a framework for addressing today's challenges in balancing quality and quantity. Whether in business, education, or personal development, balance, moderation, and continuous improvement remain vital. Industries now face the dual challenge of meeting growing demands while maintaining high standards, a balance that can be achieved through innovation, sustainability, and ethical practices.

As we move forward, these insights will serve as a foundation for exploring how modern industries and individuals can navigate the complexities of balancing these two forces, ensuring that quality and quantity are harmonized for sustainable success.

Quality and Quantity in Manufacturing

Lean Production vs. Mass Production

Origins of Lean Production

The history of Lean production is rooted in the innovative practices of the Toyota Production System (TPS), developed in mid-20th-century Japan. Emerging in a post-World War II era marked by resource scarcity and economic challenges, Lean production aimed to maximize efficiency and quality while minimizing waste. It offered a revolutionary alternative to traditional mass production methods, transforming industries worldwide.

With limited resources and intense competition, Toyota developed a system that emphasized waste elimination, continuous improvement, and respect for people. This approach aimed to enhance productivity and product quality while reducing costs. Two key figures, Taiichi Ohno and Shigeo Shingo, played instrumental roles in shaping TPS and Lean production.

Ohno, often regarded as the father of TPS, identified seven types of waste (Muda) that hinder efficiency: overproduction, waiting, transporting, over-processing, inventory, motion, and defects. His concept of "just-in-time" (JIT) production ensured materials arrived precisely when needed, reducing inventory costs and waste. Meanwhile, Shingo contributed practical tools, such as Single-Minute Exchange of Die (SMED), which minimized setup times, and Poka-Yoke, or mistake-proofing, to prevent manufacturing errors.

Ohno and Shingo's innovations created a system prioritizing continuous improvement (Kaizen) and respect for workers, fostering a culture of problem-solving and employee involvement. TPS became a global model, demonstrating that quality and efficiency are not mutually exclusive but can be achieved through thoughtful and systematic manufacturing approaches.

Core Principles of Lean Production

Lean production is guided by five core principles: value, value stream, flow, pull, and perfection. These principles form a framework for enhancing efficiency, reducing waste, and improving quality in manufacturing.

- ➢ *Value:* From the customer's perspective, value represents what the customer is willing to pay for. Lean production focuses on maximizing value-adding activities while minimizing or eliminating those that do not contribute to customer satisfaction.

- ➢ *Value Stream:* Mapping the entire process, from raw material to finished product, helps visualize where waste exists and where improvements can be made, allowing companies to streamline processes and reduce inefficiencies.

- ➢ *Flow:* Ensuring a smooth, uninterrupted flow of materials and work through production reduces bottlenecks and wait times, increasing overall efficiency and reducing lead times.

- ➢ *Pull:* Unlike traditional "push" production, where products are manufactured based on forecasts, the pull system of lean output ensures that goods are only produced when needed, based on actual demand, thereby minimizing overproduction and excess inventory.

- ➢ *Perfection:* Lean organizations continuously seek improvement, with all employees encouraged to identify inefficiencies and develop solutions. This commitment to perfection fosters constant learning and innovation.

Tools and Techniques

Several tools and techniques are integral to Lean production, helping implement its core principles.

- *5S:* A method for workplace organization, 5S ensures a clean and efficient work environment through sorting, setting in order, shining, standardizing, and sustaining the system.

- *Kaizen:* This continuous improvement philosophy encourages employees at all levels to suggest small, incremental changes that collectively lead to significant improvements in processes and procedures.

- *Kanban:* A visual scheduling system, Kanban signals when more materials or work are needed, ensuring production aligns with actual demand.

- *Jidoka,* known as *"automation with a human touch,"* empowers machines to stop production when defects are detected, allowing for immediate human intervention to address the issues.

These tools enhance efficiency and quality in manufacturing, with applications across various industries, including healthcare and logistics, demonstrating the versatility and wide-reaching impact of Lean.

The Impact on Product and Workforce

Quality Control Measures

Statistical Process Control (SPC)

Statistical Process Control (SPC) is a key methodology used to maintain and improve quality in manufacturing. By applying statistical methods to monitor and control production processes, SPC ensures that products consistently meet specified quality standards. Continuous production monitoring enables the early detection of variations, allowing for the identification of potential issues and the implementation of corrective actions before defects occur.

Role of SPC in Maintaining Quality

SPC focuses on identifying and controlling process variations, which can be categorized into two types:

- *Common Causes*: Inherent variations are due to natural fluctuations, generally stable and predictable over time.

> *Special Causes*: Unusual variations that indicate changes in the process, often due to specific issues like equipment malfunctions or human error.

By distinguishing between these two types, SPC helps manufacturers maintain process stability and intervene only when special causes arise.

Key Concepts in SPC

1. *Control Charts*: Control charts monitor process behavior over time, visually representing data points relative to control limits. These limits are calculated based on historical performance. Control charts help detect when a process is out of control and requires intervention.

Types of Control Charts:

> *X-Bar and R Charts*: Monitor the mean and range for small sample sizes.
> *P Charts*: Track the proportion of defective items.
> *C Charts*: Measure the number of defects per unit.

2. *Process Capability*: This measures how well a process operates within specification limits, using metrics such as Cp (Capability Index) and Cpk (Capability Performance Index). These metrics assess both a process's potential and actual performance.

Benefits of SPC

> Improved quality through early detection of issues.
> Cost savings by preventing defects and reducing rework.
> Increased efficiency from continuous process optimization.
> Data-driven decision-making.

Through control charts and process capability analysis, SPC is crucial in ensuring quality and efficiency in modern manufacturing.

Six Sigma

Six Sigma is a data-driven methodology designed to reduce defects and improve quality. It was first developed by Motorola in the 1980s and later popularized by companies such as General Electric. Six Sigma aims to achieve near-perfection—fewer than 3.4 defects per million opportunities.

The structured framework of Six Sigma is encapsulated in the DMAIC process, which stands for Define, Measure, Analyze, Improve, and Control. Each phase focuses on reducing variability and improving process outcomes.

1. *Define*: Identify the problem or opportunity for improvement.
2. *Measure*: Collect data to understand current performance.
3. *Analyze*: Determine the root causes of defects or inefficiencies.
4. *Improve*: Implement solutions to address root causes.
5. *Control*: Sustain improvements over time through continuous monitoring.

By following the DMAIC approach, organizations can achieve significant and sustainable improvements in quality and efficiency, positioning themselves for long-term operational excellence.

Total Quality Management (TQM)

TQM is a holistic approach that integrates quality into every aspect of an organization, emphasizing customer satisfaction, continuous improvement, and employee involvement.

Customer Satisfaction lies at the heart of TQM, which focuses on meeting or exceeding customer expectations. This is achieved through continuous feedback and rigorous adherence to quality standards.

Continuous Improvement (Kaizen) ensures that every process is regularly evaluated and enhanced. Employees across all levels are encouraged to identify inefficiencies and suggest improvements.

Employee Involvement is critical in TQM, as employees play an active role in quality improvement initiatives. This engagement creates a culture of responsibility and empowerment, improving organizational performance and job satisfaction.

TQM fosters a culture of excellence that supports long-term success by integrating customer feedback, continuous improvement, and employee participation.

Workforce Implications

Employee Engagement and Satisfaction

Lean principles, particularly respect for people and continuous improvement, significantly enhance employee engagement and satisfaction. By empowering employees to take ownership of their work, collaborate cross-functionally, and engage in ongoing learning, a culture of innovation and engagement is fostered.

Lean practices encourage:

- *Empowerment*: Giving employees decision-making authority.
- *Collaboration*: Breaking down silos and fostering teamwork.
- *Recognition*: Regularly acknowledging employee contributions.

As demonstrated by the Toyota Production System, these principles foster an environment where employees feel valued and motivated, ultimately contributing to the overall success of the organization.

Skill Development

Lean environments emphasize cross-training and continuous learning, enhancing workforce flexibility and problem-solving capabilities. Cross-training allows employees to perform multiple roles, fostering operational resilience and efficiency.

In contrast, mass production environments often focus on specialization, which can increase productivity but reduce flexibility and job satisfaction. By promoting continuous skill development, Lean organizations ensure a more dynamic and engaged workforce better positioned for long-term success.

Workplace Safety and Ergonomics

Lean's focus on waste elimination extends to improving safety and ergonomics. By fostering a culture of continuous improvement and utilizing tools like 5S (Sort, Set in Order, Shine, Standardize, Sustain),

Quality verses Quantity: Is There a Middle Way?

Lean organizations proactively address safety issues, resulting in safer and more organized workspaces.

Mass production environments, on the other hand, may pose ergonomic risks due to repetitive tasks, though advancements in automation can help mitigate these issues.

Balancing Efficiency and Excellence

Case studies of successful implementation, such as the Toyota Production System (TPS), demonstrate how Lean principles can balance efficiency with high-quality outcomes. Toyota's use of Just-in-Time (JIT) and Jidoka (a form of automation that incorporates human intervention) has set global standards for manufacturing excellence.

Similarly, BMW's integration of advanced technology and rigorous quality control ensures that high production volumes do not compromise its commitment to premium quality. On the other hand, Tesla's early production struggles with the Model 3 highlighted the challenges of over-automation and underscored the importance of striking a balance between speed and quality.

Innovation and Continuous Improvement

The concept of *Kaizen* underlines the power of minor, incremental improvements that collectively lead to significant gains in efficiency and quality. Organizations across various industries, from automotive to healthcare, have successfully implemented Kaizen principles to drive continuous innovation.

Technologies such as automation, AI, and IoT enhance manufacturing processes by improving predictive maintenance, reducing human error, and facilitating real-time decision-making.

Future Trends and Opportunities

Sustainable Manufacturing

Green manufacturing practices are becoming a priority as companies strive to reduce their environmental impact. Waste reduction, energy efficiency, and the use of eco-friendly materials are central to this shift, supported by technologies such as 3D printing and digital twins that optimize resource use and minimize waste.

Circular Economy

The circular economy model encourages the design of products for longevity, reusability, and recyclability. Companies like Philips and Renault lead the way by adopting closed-loop systems, where waste is minimized and resources are continually reused.

Customization and Flexibility

Mass customization enables companies to deliver tailored products at scale, combining efficiency with personalization. Examples from Nike, Dell, and BMW demonstrate how mass customization can meet customer demands without compromising operational efficiency.

Agile Manufacturing

Agile manufacturing emphasizes flexibility and the ability to respond rapidly to market changes. Companies like Zara and Tesla illustrate the benefits of agile practices in adapting to evolving consumer preferences and technological advancements.

Reflection on Manufacturing Practices

Chapter 2 explored the balance between efficiency and quality in manufacturing. Manufacturers can achieve operational excellence through various methodologies like Lean, Six Sigma, and TQM, as well as the integration of advanced technologies. The future of manufacturing lies in the continued pursuit of sustainability, customization, and workforce empowerment, ensuring that efficiency and quality remain mutually reinforcing goals.

Quality verses Quantity: Is There a Middle Way?

High-Quality Products vs. Market Share

By highlighting how businesses face this challenge, we can emphasize the core tension between quality and scaling. It's key to make this section about showing the trade-offs and how leaders overcome them.

Refined version: In the business world, there is often a perceived trade-off between pursuing high-quality products and expanding market share. The assumption is that focusing too much on quality can limit growth due to the higher costs of producing premium products. However, this tension is increasingly being challenged by businesses recognizing that quality and market share are not mutually exclusive. Companies like Apple and Toyota have proven that a relentless focus on quality can drive market expansion, as customer satisfaction, brand loyalty, and reputation for excellence fuel repeat business and organic growth. By setting industry standards for innovation and product excellence, these companies demonstrate that quality can be a powerful growth engine rather than a hindrance to market share.

Strategies for Balancing Quality and Quantity

We can streamline this by making each point stand out as a unique strategy with a clear benefit. Let's make the connections between quality, scaling, and the benefits of each strategy even more direct.

Customer-Centric Approaches:

A customer-first mindset is crucial for businesses aiming to strike a balance between quality and quantity. By deeply understanding customer needs, companies can tailor their production processes to deliver high-quality products while scaling to meet demand. This approach involves constant communication with customers through feedback loops, which enables businesses to innovate and improve without losing sight of what matters most to the customer. For instance, when a company aligns its quality standards with customer expectations, it builds trust, encourages repeat purchases and brand loyalty, and supports growth and product excellence. Companies like Patagonia, which prioritize customer satisfaction, demonstrate that maintaining high standards can coexist with strategic growth.

Innovation and Differentiation:

Innovation and differentiation are crucial in striking a balance between quality and quantity in a rapidly evolving business landscape. Innovation enables businesses to integrate the latest technologies and best practices, enhancing both the quality of their products and the efficiency of their production processes. For example, the tech industry thrives on constant innovation, with companies like Tesla continuously pushing the boundaries of what's possible while maintaining strict quality controls. Differentiation enables businesses to establish a unique market position, attracting consumers who value their distinct approach. This can be achieved through product features, branding, or sustainability practices, as seen in companies like Patagonia, which leverages its commitment to environmental responsibility to differentiate itself from competitors.

Scalable Quality:

Scalable quality refers to a business's ability to grow while maintaining the high standards that define its brand. This can be achieved through standardized processes, automation, and a strong supply chain, all of which ensure consistency regardless of production scale. Lean manufacturing, for example, plays a crucial role in scaling quality, as demonstrated by Toyota's Just-In-Time production system. This system allows Toyota to respond to demand efficiently without sacrificing the high quality that has become synonymous with its brand. Scalable quality is essential for long-term growth, as it enables businesses to expand without diluting their core values or compromising the integrity of their products.

Case Studies: Industry Leaders

This section can be tightened by focusing on how these companies practically integrate quality and market share strategies, highlighting the results.

Apple:

Apple has achieved a balance between high-quality products and market share by prioritizing design excellence and innovation. The company's ability to deliver cutting-edge technology while maintaining simplicity in design has set it apart from competitors. Apple's seamless ecosystem of products also ensures that customers stay within its network, driving repeat business and expanding its market presence. Apple's dedication to strict quality controls and supply chain management allows the company to scale production without sacrificing the premium experience its customers expect.

Toyota:

Toyota's Lean principles have revolutionized the way businesses approach large-scale production and quality. By implementing the Toyota Production System, the company has successfully reduced waste and increased efficiency, while ensuring that its vehicles meet the highest standards of reliability and performance. Toyota's commitment to continuous improvement and its Just-In-Time production system has allowed it to maintain quality at scale, ensuring customer satisfaction and brand loyalty.

Patagonia:

Patagonia's commitment to sustainability has defined its brand and enabled it to grow without compromising quality. Patagonia has cultivated a loyal customer base that values ethical business practices by focusing on environmental responsibility and durable, high-quality products. The company's innovative approach to sustainability, such as its Worn Wear program, further reinforces its reputation for quality and integrity, driving customer loyalty and market growth.

Balancing Innovation and Execution

In business, striking a balance between innovation and execution is crucial. While innovation drives growth and market differentiation, execution ensures that these innovations are brought to life effectively, maintaining quality and meeting customer expectations. The challenge for many businesses lies in not letting the pursuit of innovation overshadow the importance of flawless execution. Companies that excel in balancing both can introduce groundbreaking products and services without compromising on the operational excellence needed to scale these innovations.

Continuous Improvement and Kaizen

The Japanese philosophy of Kaizen, which translates to "continuous improvement," is a fundamental principle for businesses seeking to enhance efficiency, productivity, and quality. Kaizen emphasizes making small, consistent changes rather than pursuing radical overhauls. This philosophy promotes a proactive approach to problem-solving, where all employees—from executives to frontline staff—are involved in enhancing processes and outcomes.

The core principles of Kaizen include continuous improvement, employee involvement, standardization, waste elimination, quality at the source, and workforce empowerment through training. These principles foster a culture where employees are encouraged and expected to suggest and implement changes, resulting in gradual yet impactful improvements throughout the organization.

For example, Toyota, the birthplace of Kaizen, utilizes the "Andon" system, which allows workers to stop production at the first sign of a defect and address issues in real-time. In the healthcare industry, Virginia Mason Medical Center in Seattle has implemented Kaizen to streamline patient care, reducing wait times and improving patient satisfaction. These examples demonstrate how the principles of Kaizen can be applied across various industries to maintain high standards of quality while enhancing efficiency.

Implementing Kaizen

Implementing Kaizen requires a structured approach, beginning with comprehensive employee training. Employees must be equipped with problem-solving techniques, such as the Plan-Do-Check-Act (PDCA) cycle, and Lean tools, including 5S and value stream mapping. This knowledge empowers them to take ownership of continuous improvement initiatives, enabling them to drive improvements.

Cross-functional teams, often referred to as Kaizen teams, are crucial to the process. These teams, comprising employees from various levels and departments, collaborate to identify inefficiencies, develop solutions, and implement improvements. Kaizen events, or "blitzes," provide short, intensive problem-solving sessions that yield immediate, tangible results.

Tools like the PDCA cycle and regular review cycles ensure that changes are sustained and new improvement opportunities are continually identified. Leadership plays a critical role in fostering a culture that supports these continuous improvement efforts, providing the necessary resources and encouragement for long-term success.

For example, General Electric (GE) has successfully implemented Kaizen by forming cross-functional teams and establishing rigorous review cycles to address operational inefficiencies. Similarly, Ritz-Carlton empowers its employees to suggest service improvements, enhancing operational efficiency and customer satisfaction.

Quality Management Systems (QMS)

A robust Quality Management System (QMS) is crucial for any business aiming to uphold high-quality standards while expanding its operations. ISO 9001, part of the ISO 9000 family, is one of the most recognized frameworks for establishing and maintaining a QMS. The ISO 9001 standard emphasizes leadership commitment, customer focus, a process-driven approach, and risk-based thinking.

Adopting ISO 9001 ensures that quality becomes a consistent aspect of a business's operations. Processes are standardized, documented, and continually reviewed to drive improvements. This consistency enhances product and service quality, building customer trust.

Alongside ISO 9001, businesses may adopt other standards to address specific areas, such as ISO 14001 for environmental management or ISO 45001 for health and safety. For example, Siemens uses ISO 9001 to streamline its global manufacturing processes, ensuring its products meet stringent quality standards across diverse markets.

Six Sigma

Six Sigma is a structured, data-driven methodology focused on reducing defects and improving quality. Developed by Motorola and popularized by General Electric, it aims for near-perfect quality, targeting a defect rate of no more than 3.4 defects per million opportunities. Six Sigma relies on two key processes: DMAIC (Define, Measure, Analyze, Improve, Control) for improving existing processes and DMADV (Define, Measure, Analyze, Design, Verify) for developing new products or processes.

Six Sigma tools, such as control charts, root cause analysis, and Failure Mode and Effects Analysis (FMEA), enable businesses to systematically identify and eliminate sources of errors and variability. Companies like GE and Ford have successfully applied this methodology to reduce defects and drive significant improvements in quality.

Resource Allocation and Efficiency

Effective resource allocation is crucial for striking a balance between quality and quantity. Businesses must optimize their use of time, labor, capital, and materials to maintain high standards while meeting production demands. Lean manufacturing principles, which focus on eliminating waste and improving efficiency, play a critical role in this process.

Companies like Toyota have adopted Lean principles. Toyota utilizes just-in-time production to ensure resources are allocated efficiently, eliminating overproduction and excess inventory. Advanced data analytics and predictive modeling also help businesses like General

Electric optimize resource allocation, enabling them to predict equipment failures and streamline supply chain management.

As seen at Starbucks, strategic workforce management ensures employees are trained and aligned with the company's operational goals, enhancing quality and efficiency. Flexible manufacturing systems, such as Dell's build-to-order model, enable businesses to quickly customize products without compromising quality.

Lean Manufacturing

Lean manufacturing, rooted in the Toyota Production System, emphasizes waste reduction, value-added activities, employee empowerment, and continuous improvement. By systematically eliminating waste in overproduction, defects, and excess inventory, businesses can streamline their operations, reduce costs, and improve product quality.

Case studies from companies like Danaher and Nike demonstrate the transformative power of Lean. Danaher's use of Lean tools such as 5S and Kanban has driven efficiency and quality across its diverse portfolio. At the same time, Nike's application of Lean in its supply chain has reduced lead times and improved operational flexibility.

Future Trends and Opportunities

As the business landscape evolves, technological advancements and sustainability initiatives reshape how companies balance quality and quantity. The future presents significant business opportunities to harness these developments, ensuring operational efficiency and product excellence.

Technological Advancements

Automation and AI

Automation and artificial intelligence (AI) are becoming integral to modern business operations, enhancing productivity, quality control, and decision-making. Automation, which relies on advanced machinery and robotics, enables continuous, error-free operations, while AI processes large datasets to provide insights that drive more innovative business strategies. These technologies are revolutionizing industries by streamlining operations and freeing up human resources to focus on strategic tasks.

In manufacturing, automation improves precision and output, as demonstrated by Tesla's use of robotics in its Gigafactories. This level of automation allows the company to scale production while maintaining stringent quality standards. Similarly, Amazon's use of robotics and automated systems in logistics ensures efficiency and accuracy, enabling the company to handle high volumes of orders while delivering products quickly and reliably.

AI enhances business processes through predictive maintenance and data-driven decision-making. For instance, General Electric (GE) uses AI to analyze data from industrial machines, predicting potential failures before they occur and ensuring continuous, high-quality production. In retail, companies like Walmart utilize AI to optimize inventory management, ensuring that products are available when needed while minimizing excess stock and associated costs.

These technologies also play a crucial role in quality control. AI-powered vision systems, like those used by Siemens, can detect minute defects that human inspectors might miss, ensuring that only top-quality products reach the market. Integrating automation and AI enhances efficiency and elevates quality, laying the groundwork for sustained business growth.

Industry 4.0

Industry 4.0, also known as the Fourth Industrial Revolution, represents a shift toward smart factories and fully integrated digital ecosystems. This concept hinges on technologies like the Internet of Things (IoT), big data analytics, AI, and cloud computing, enabling real-time monitoring and optimization of production processes.

In smart factories, interconnected machines and sensors collect data at every stage of production, enabling businesses to identify and resolve issues before they escalate. For instance, Siemens' Amberg Electronics

Plant operates with a high level of automation and connectivity, maintaining near-zero defects and exceptional productivity.

The potential of Industry 4.0 extends beyond the manufacturing sector. Through digital integration across the supply chain, companies like BMW synchronize production with their suppliers, ensuring the timely delivery of components and reducing inventory costs. Big data analytics, such as GE's Predix platform, further enhance these processes by predicting maintenance needs, optimizing production schedules, and improving decision-making.

The flexibility of Industry 4.0 also enables customization at scale, utilizing technologies such as 3D printing to produce personalized products without compromising quality. This level of innovation enables businesses to remain agile in responding to market changes while maintaining high standards.

Sustainable Practices

Green Business Models

Sustainability is a key ethical consideration and a driving force behind innovation and long-term business success. Green business models focus on minimizing environmental impact while maintaining profitability, and many companies are adopting circular economy principles to achieve this balance.

The circular economy emphasizes designing products for durability, reparability, and recyclability, keeping materials in use for as long as possible. Patagonia's Worn Wear program exemplifies this approach, encouraging customers to repair and recycle their gear, thus extending product life and reducing waste. Similarly, Interface, a global carpet manufacturer, utilizes recycled materials and operates a take-back program, recycling old carpets into new products, demonstrating how sustainability can drive innovation and lead to cost savings.

Tesla's electric vehicles demonstrate how sustainable practices can drive industry transformation. By focusing on renewable energy and reducing greenhouse gas emissions, Tesla has proven that sustainability can fuel market growth and profitability.

Circular Economy

The circular economy model represents a shift from the traditional take-make-dispose economy to one where resources are reused and regenerated. This approach enhances both quality and quantity by prioritizing durability and recyclability.

As seen with Patagonia's durable outdoor gear, businesses are rethinking product design to ensure longevity and repairability. Companies like Apple also adopt take-back programs, recycling old devices into new products to minimize the need for raw materials.

Product-as-a-service models, where businesses retain ownership of their products and offer them as a service, further support this shift. For example, Philips' lighting-as-a-service model reduces waste by ensuring that products are maintained and upgraded as needed while still meeting customer needs.

This way, the circular economy promotes sustainable practices while enabling businesses to maintain large-scale production.

Reflection on Business Practices

This chapter has explored the delicate balance between quality and quantity in business. Achieving this balance requires strategic foresight, a commitment to continuous improvement, and an openness to innovation. Companies that prioritize customer-centric approaches, foster a culture of innovation, and invest in scalable quality processes will be well-positioned for sustainable success.

Customer satisfaction remains at the heart of quality-driven business strategies. By focusing on customer needs, businesses can tailor their products and services to meet market demands while maintaining high standards. Meanwhile, innovation and differentiation allow companies to stay ahead of the competition, offering unique products that meet customer expectations.

We also explored how scalable quality processes, such as those employed by Toyota, enable businesses to grow while maintaining high quality standards. The importance of leadership in maintaining this balance was further demonstrated through case studies of companies like Apple, Toyota, and Patagonia.

However, businesses must also remain vigilant of the common pitfalls associated with rapid growth, such as overemphasizing speed at the expense of quality. The failures of companies like Boeing and General Motors underscore the importance of rigorous quality control and the importance of listening to customer feedback.

Implications for Future Business

Integrating automation, AI, and Industry 4.0 technologies will be pivotal in shaping business operations. These advancements enable businesses to achieve both efficiency and precision, resulting in higher-quality products at scale. Similarly, adopting sustainable practices and circular economy principles will become increasingly important as consumers and regulators demand more environmentally responsible business models.

In this evolving landscape, businesses must continue to innovate, adopt sustainable practices, and maintain a relentless focus on quality. By doing so, they can meet the challenges of tomorrow's market while delivering the high standards that customers expect.

Quality verses Quantity: Is There a Middle Way?

Quality and Quantity in Retail

Customer Experience vs. Sales Volume

Balancing customer satisfaction with sales targets is a constant challenge for retailers. To navigate this tension, personalization and customization have become effective strategies, creating a more engaging shopping experience while driving higher sales volumes. Retailers utilize data analytics and AI to tailor their offerings to individual customer preferences, thereby significantly enhancing customer satisfaction. For instance, Amazon's recommendation system, powered by sophisticated algorithms, delivers personalized product suggestions based on past behavior, creating a tailored shopping journey that fosters loyalty and increases sales. Similarly, Stitch Fix utilizes AI to provide personalized fashion advice. These curating clothing selections resonate with individual tastes, while Sephora's Color IQ technology personalizes beauty product recommendations to match skin tones, driving both customer satisfaction and repeat purchases. These retailers illustrate how personalization can simultaneously fulfill customer desires and meet sales targets, demonstrating the potential for a win-win situation.

Case Studies: Successful Retailers

Zara exemplifies the delicate balance between speed and quality through its fast-fashion model. The brand's success lies in its highly efficient supply chain, which enables it to translate fashion trends into retail products swiftly. Zara achieves unparalleled speed by combining in-house production with strategic supplier relationships while maintaining quality. Frequent restocking of stores with fresh designs, combined with data analytics to adjust inventory, ensures customer satisfaction while minimizing waste and overproduction.

On the other hand, Nordstrom prioritizes high-quality products and exceptional customer service. Its "customer-first" philosophy is evident in personalized shopping experiences, flexible return policies, and a highly curated product selection. This focus on quality extends to every aspect of the retail experience, fostering a deep sense of customer loyalty. Nordstrom's loyalty program further strengthens its customer base, while its seamless integration of online and offline channels ensures a consistent and high-quality shopping experience.

Costco, known for its bulk-buying strategy, strikes a remarkable balance between offering high-quality products and maintaining cost-effectiveness. By focusing on volume sales through its membership model, Costco can negotiate better prices with suppliers and pass the savings on to consumers. Kirkland Signature, a brand known for offering premium quality at lower prices, reinforces Costco's commitment to quality without compromising affordability. Efficient supply chain management is crucial, enabling Costco to provide fresh products consistently while keeping costs low.

Lean Retail

Retailers have increasingly adopted Lean principles to optimize operations and improve efficiency. Lean principles—value, value stream, flow, pull, and perfection—reduce waste and streamline processes to enhance efficiency. Retailers such as Walmart and Target have implemented these methodologies to strengthen their operations, thereby improving customer satisfaction while reducing costs. Continuous improvement (Kaizen), 5S (Sort, Set in Order, Shine, Standardize, Sustain), and Just-In-Time (JIT) inventory management have allowed these retailers to minimize excess inventory, reduce waste, and improve overall efficiency, ultimately benefiting both the retailer and the customer.

Just-In-Time (JIT) Inventory Management

The concept of JIT involves ordering and receiving products only as needed, directly aligning supply with demand. This approach minimizes inventory costs, reduces the need for extensive storage, and ensures that products are available when customers want them. JIT has proven highly effective for retailers such as Walmart, which utilizes real-time sales data to restock items, ensuring that fresh products are always available while avoiding overstocking. JIT requires precise demand forecasting and strong supplier relationships. While it offers significant benefits, such as reduced carrying costs and improved cash flow, it also presents challenges, including supply chain disruptions and the need for reliable suppliers.

Case Studies: Lean Retail Implementations

Walmart and Amazon serve as prime examples of Lean retail practices in action. Walmart has used continuous improvement, JIT inventory management, and value stream mapping to optimize its supply chain, ensuring high product availability and minimizing costs. Amazon's fulfillment centers employ Lean methodologies alongside cutting-edge automation, allowing for rapid delivery, reduced waste, and an enhanced customer experience.

Challenges and Opportunities

Retailers often face challenges when balancing product variety and quality. A diverse product range can complicate inventory management and supplier relationships, while inconsistent quality standards can damage a brand's reputation. To address these challenges, retailers must adopt rigorous quality control measures, leverage data analytics for accurate demand forecasting, and foster strong supplier relationships. Furthermore, supply chain management in a global context requires careful navigation of regional regulations, logistical challenges, and quality control across geographically dispersed suppliers. Blockchain can enhance supply chain transparency and ensure product quality throughout the supply chain.

Opportunities for Improvement

Technological innovation continues to offer opportunities for improvement in retail. Predictive analytics, AI, and the Internet of Things (IoT) allow retailers to optimize inventory management, personalize customer experiences, and improve supply chain transparency. Automated warehouses, AI-driven personalization, and smart shelves are transforming the industry, enabling more efficient operations and enhanced customer satisfaction.

Sustainable Retail Practices

Sustainability is becoming increasingly important in the retail sector. Green business models prioritize reducing environmental impact and are now essential for achieving long-term success. Companies like Patagonia, IKEA, and Walmart have demonstrated that sustainability can drive innovation and brand loyalty while reducing operational costs. Fairtrade and ethical sourcing are equally important, ensuring that products are made under fair working conditions and with minimal environmental impact. Retailers like Starbucks and Ben & Jerry's promote ethical practices, enhancing product quality and social responsibility.

Enhancing Customer Experience

Customer feedback is a vital tool for maintaining high-quality retail experiences. Retailers that actively collect and act on customer insights can continuously improve their offerings, thereby enhancing customer satisfaction and loyalty. Starbucks, Amazon, and Walmart exemplify how retailers utilize customer feedback to drive continuous improvement, refining everything from product offerings to in-store experiences.

Innovative Retail Concepts

Omnichannel retail, which integrates physical and digital shopping experiences, is becoming the standard in retail. Companies like Nordstrom, Walmart, and Sephora have developed successful omnichannel strategies that provide a seamless customer journey and ensure consistent shopping experiences across all platforms. Experiential retail is also growing, with brands like Apple and Nike offering immersive store experiences that deepen customer engagement and build stronger brand connections.

Future Trends and Opportunities

Technological advancements, including AI, machine learning, AR, and VR, are revolutionizing retail, enabling more personalized, efficient, and

Quality verses Quantity: Is There a Middle Way?

immersive shopping experiences. Sustainability and ethical practices will also continue to shape the future of retail, as consumers demand more environmentally responsible and ethically produced goods. Retailers that embrace these trends will be well-positioned for future success.

Retailers face the ongoing challenge of balancing quality and quantity while meeting consumer expectations and maintaining operational efficiency. By implementing Lean principles, leveraging technology, and committing to sustainability, retailers can achieve this balance, ensuring a satisfying and responsible shopping experience. As the retail landscape continues to evolve, businesses that integrate these practices will be better positioned to thrive now and in the future. This chapter sets the foundation for exploring these trends and practices across other industries in subsequent chapters.

Quality verses Quantity: Is There a Middle Way?

Quality vs. Quantity in Product Development

Introduction

The delicate balance between quality and quantity has become a defining factor in business success within the rapidly evolving product development landscape. As consumers become more discerning and market competition intensifies, companies must carefully navigate the tension between producing high-quality products and meeting the demand for scale. This chapter examines the intricate dynamics of quality and quantity in product development, exploring strategies, historical perspectives, and modern methodologies that enable businesses to strike this balance effectively.

Quality and quantity are not mutually exclusive; however, the challenge lies in striking the right balance. High-quality products cultivate consumer trust and brand loyalty, reflecting a company's commitment to excellence. However, focusing solely on quality can lead to slower production cycles, higher costs, and reduced responsiveness to market demands. On the other hand, prioritizing quantity enables companies to meet growing consumer demand and benefit from economies of scale, but at the risk of compromising the product's integrity. This chapter examines how businesses can effectively integrate the best of both worlds—delivering high-quality products at scale while maintaining innovation, efficiency, and consumer satisfaction.

We will examine real-world examples, industry best practices, and the historical evolution of product development to uncover how companies have successfully navigated these challenges. Lean, Six Sigma, and other frameworks will be discussed alongside the role of innovation and leadership in fostering a culture that values quality and quantity.

Ultimately, this chapter will provide insights and tools to help businesses assess and apply the optimal balance within their unique contexts.

Historical Context

The struggle to balance quality and quantity in product development is not a new challenge; it has shaped business strategies since the dawn of the industrial era. The Industrial Revolution marked a pivotal moment, as mechanized production enabled companies to meet growing demand on an unprecedented scale. However, this shift from craftsmanship to mass production often led to a compromise in quality, sparking the first debates on the trade-offs between these two forces.

One of the most iconic historical examples is the Ford Motor Company in the early 20th century. Henry Ford's assembly line revolutionized production, drastically increasing efficiency and lowering costs. The Model T became a symbol of affordable mass production. However, this relentless focus on standardization and speed led to limitations in customization and quality, eventually causing consumer dissatisfaction as competitors emerged with more refined options.

In contrast, the post-World War II era witnessed the rise of Japanese manufacturing, which offered a distinct perspective on the balance between quality and quantity. Companies like Toyota adopted Total Quality Management (TQM) and Just-In-Time (JIT) production, focusing on continuous improvement and waste reduction. This approach demonstrated that it was possible to maintain high quality while scaling production, thereby setting new global standards for the industry.

The technology boom of the late 20th and early 21st centuries added further complexity to the equation. Companies like Apple and Microsoft have had to balance the rapid delivery of innovative products with maintaining high-quality standards. Apple's emphasis on design excellence, product reliability, and seamless production scaling exemplifies how companies can simultaneously manage quality and quantity. These historical lessons provide valuable insights into how businesses today can learn from past successes and failures to strike the right balance in product development.

Craftsmanship vs. Mass Production

Craftsmanship Defined

Craftsmanship embodies the pinnacle of quality in product development, emphasizing skill, precision, and artistic excellence. It involves meticulous attention to detail, a deep understanding of materials, and a commitment to creating products that are not only functional but also aesthetically pleasing and durable. This dedication to excellence transcends mere functionality, producing goods that stand the test of time.

The essence of craftsmanship lies in the time and care invested in each product. Unlike mass production, which prioritizes speed and volume, craftsmanship values thorough inspection and refinement at every stage of the process. Skilled artisans, often with years of training and experience, devote themselves to ensuring that each item is crafted to the highest standards. This personal touch imbues products with uniqueness, setting them apart from the uniformity of mass-produced goods.

For example, a handmade leather bag or a finely crafted piece of furniture showcases superior craftsmanship and is valuable due to the time and skill involved. While this approach may not yield high volumes, it offers unparalleled quality that resonates with consumers seeking durability, individuality, and beauty.

The Dynamics of Mass Production

On the other hand, mass production focuses on efficiency, cost reduction, and the ability to produce large quantities of goods rapidly. The industrialization of production processes has enabled companies to meet increasing demand while lowering costs, making products more accessible to a broader consumer base.

However, this focus on quantity often comes at the expense of quality. The need for speed and volume can lead to shortcuts in material selection, design, and production processes, which may compromise the durability and aesthetic appeal of the final product. The fast fashion industry, exemplified by brands like Zara and H&M, illustrates the trade-offs inherent in mass production. These companies quickly translate runway trends into affordable, ready-to-wear garments, but often at the cost of longevity and sustainability.

Mass production remains essential for industries where scale is necessary to meet demand and maintain profitability. The challenge lies in finding ways to incorporate elements of craftsmanship into mass production processes, thereby achieving both quality and quantity.

Case Studies: Craftsmanship and Mass Production

Let's examine a few notable examples to illustrate the balance between craftsmanship and mass production. Luxury brands such as Hermès and Patek Philippe epitomize the highest standards of craftsmanship. Hermès' dedication to artisanal techniques and meticulous attention to detail, particularly in their Birkin and Kelly bags, ensures that each product is a masterpiece, taking up to 18 hours to complete. Similarly, Patek Philippe, known for its intricately handcrafted timepieces, exemplifies the pinnacle of precision and luxury.

In contrast, mass-production giants like Zara and H&M operate at the opposite end of the spectrum. Zara's vertically integrated supply chain enables rapid production and distribution, allowing it to keep up with ever-changing fashion trends at a lower price point. However, this speed and efficiency come at the cost of product longevity and quality, highlighting the compromises made in favor of quantity.

Some companies, like Tesla, seek to bridge this divide by combining the innovation and precision of craftsmanship with the scalability of modern manufacturing. Tesla's electric vehicles are renowned for their advanced technology and high quality; however, the company has also prioritized scaling production to meet increasing demand.

Quality verses Quantity: Is There a Middle Way?
Consumer Preferences: Navigating Quality vs. Quantity

Consumer preferences are fluid and shaped by economic conditions, cultural trends, and technological advancements. In times of economic prosperity, consumers are more likely to prioritize quality and are willing to invest in premium products that offer longevity and status. Conversely, quantity takes precedence during economic downturns as consumers seek affordability and practicality.

The rise of sustainability movements has also influenced consumer behavior, with a growing emphasis on ethical consumption and environmental responsibility. Brands that focus on craftsmanship, sustainable sourcing, and quality, such as Patagonia and Everlane, have capitalized on this shift, appealing to consumers who value long-lasting, ethically produced goods over fast fashion or disposable products.

Technology has further empowered consumers to make informed choices, as online reviews, social media, and e-commerce platforms provide transparency and accessibility. Consumers can now easily research products and compare quality, making them more discerning in their purchasing decisions.

Ethical Implications: Sustainability and Labor Practices

The balance between quality and quantity in product development also has significant ethical implications, particularly concerning sustainability and labor practices. Mass production has a substantial environmental impact, with industries such as fast fashion contributing to pollution, resource depletion, and waste.

On the other hand, high-quality, durable products offer a more sustainable alternative. Products designed for longevity require fewer replacements, reducing the overall demand for raw materials and minimizing waste. Brands that prioritize sustainability, such as Patagonia, encourage consumers to repair and reuse their products, aligning with the principles of a circular economy.

Labor practices in mass production are another critical concern. Low wages, poor working conditions, and long hours are often hallmarks of industries focused on producing large quantities of goods at low costs. In contrast, companies that emphasize craftsmanship typically provide fair wages and better working conditions, fostering a more ethical approach to production.

Corporate Responsibility and Product Lifecycle Management

Corporate social responsibility (CSR) plays a pivotal role in striking a balance between quality and quantity. Companies like Patagonia, Tesla, and Lush have successfully integrated CSR into their product development strategies by focusing on sustainable sourcing, eco-friendly production, and fair labor practices. These companies demonstrate that it is possible to produce high-quality products while maintaining ethical and sustainable practices.

Product lifecycle management (PLM) further supports this balance by managing a product from conception to disposal. PLM tools ensure that products are designed for scalability without compromising quality and that sustainability is considered at every stage, from material sourcing to end-of-life recycling.

Balancing Craftsmanship and Mass Production: Strategies for Integration

Companies are adopting innovative strategies, such as mass customization, flexible manufacturing systems, and Lean manufacturing, to strike a balance between craftsmanship and mass production. Mass customization enables businesses to offer personalized products on a large scale, while flexible manufacturing systems allow for rapid adaptation to changes in design and production volume. Lean manufacturing, which emphasizes waste reduction and process optimization, ensures that quality is maintained even in high-volume production environments.

Balancing quality and quantity in product development is a continuous challenge that necessitates a thoughtful strategy, innovation, and effective leadership. By integrating the principles of craftsmanship with the efficiency of mass production, businesses can produce high-quality products at scale, meeting consumer expectations while maintaining

Quality verses Quantity: Is There a Middle Way?

profitability and sustainability. This balance will remain a cornerstone of successful product development as industries evolve.

Quality verses Quantity: Is There a Middle Way?

Quality and Quantity in Personal Development and Lifestyle Choices

Prioritization and Time Management

One of the key strategies for achieving work-life balance is effective prioritization and time management. Techniques like the Eisenhower Matrix can help individuals categorize tasks based on urgency and importance. This method encourages focusing on important but not urgent tasks, preventing last-minute stress while allowing space for long-term planning and self-care. Another approach is time blocking, where specific hours are dedicated to work and personal activities, allowing for focused attention on each area without overlap. The Pomodoro Technique can also be effective, breaking work into intervals (usually 25 minutes) followed by short breaks. This structured approach fosters productivity while ensuring work does not bleed into personal time.

Setting Boundaries

Setting boundaries is crucial for maintaining a healthy work-life balance. Defining and sticking to work hours creates a clear line between work and personal life. To reinforce these boundaries physically, creating a dedicated workspace—whether at home or in an office can be beneficial. This separation allows for mental shifts between work mode and relaxation, ensuring that work stress does not interfere with personal time. Tips for maintaining boundaries include communicating expectations with colleagues and family, taking scheduled breaks, and disconnecting from work-related communications after hours.

When combined, these strategies enable individuals to manage their time and energy more effectively, striking a balance between the demands of work and the need for personal fulfillment.

Mindfulness Practices

Mindfulness is a powerful tool for staying grounded in the present moment and managing stress. Practices such as meditation, deep breathing exercises, and mindful walking can significantly enhance an individual's awareness of their mental and physical state. Meditation, even for a few minutes daily, helps calm the mind and cultivate focus, allowing individuals to approach tasks more clearly. Deep breathing exercise, particularly in moments of stress, can lower anxiety levels and create a sense of calm. Mindful walking, where one pays close attention to the sensations of walking, the environment, and breathing, encourages people to slow down and fully engage with their surroundings. These practices enhance mental well-being and improve productivity and quality of life by helping individuals remain present and focused on tasks, thereby reducing feelings of overwhelm.

Intentional Living

Intentional living involves making conscious choices that reflect one's values and long-term goals rather than reacting passively to life's demands. It emphasizes quality over the mere accumulation of tasks or material goods, encouraging people to focus on what truly matters to them. For example, someone practicing intentional living might prioritize spending time with family over working late, knowing that these moments contribute to their happiness and fulfillment. Individuals can find purpose and meaning in their work and personal lives by aligning daily actions with core values. This balance improves the quality of life and enhances the quantity of meaningful experiences, leading to a richer, more fulfilling existence.

In essence, mindfulness and intentional living provide a pathway to achieving balance, enabling individuals to cultivate both quality and quantity in their daily lives.

Principles of Minimalism

At the heart of minimalism is valuing experiences over material possessions. Minimalism encourages individuals to strip away excess and focus on what truly matters, whether personal relationships, self-growth, or meaningful experiences. Reducing physical clutter often leads to a clearer mental state, which in turn fosters better decision-making and reduces stress. The "less is more" principle is central to minimalism, as it invites people to live intentionally, making room for higher-quality experiences by eliminating distractions. Minimalism also promotes sustainability, as reducing consumption naturally produces less waste and a smaller environmental footprint. The benefits of this lifestyle include enhanced mental clarity, improved emotional well-being, and a more profound sense of fulfillment.

Minimalist Practices

Adopting a minimalist lifestyle requires practical changes that align with the philosophy of simplicity. One key practice is decluttering, which involves systematically going through one's belongings and removing items that no longer serve a purpose or bring joy. This process frees up physical and mental space, as the individual no longer has to manage or worry about excess possessions. Simplifying routines is another approach, where individuals streamline their daily tasks and focus on the essentials, thereby reducing the mental load associated with decision-making. Mindful consumption is equally important, encouraging people to buy only what they truly need and to invest in quality items that will last longer. This shift in mindset fosters a greater appreciation for the things one owns and the experiences one prioritizes.

These minimalist principles and practices empower individuals to lead more intentional lives, focusing on the quality of experience rather than the quantity of possessions. This ultimately contributes to personal well-being and a more sustainable way of life.

Consumerism and Quality of Life

Consumerism often promotes the idea that happiness and success are tied to acquiring material possessions. In a consumer-driven culture, people are encouraged to buy more, with the promise that owning more will enhance their quality of life. However, this endless pursuit of material goods can lead to stress, financial strain, and dissatisfaction as the temporary joy of acquiring new items quickly fades. The constant bombardment of advertising and social pressures to keep up with trends can make it difficult to find contentment in what one already has, leading to a cycle of overconsumption and disappointment. Consumerism can also impact mental health, as individuals may feel overwhelmed by the clutter and maintenance of their possessions or become trapped in a comparison-driven mindset.

Finding Balance

Balancing consumerism with minimalism offers a way to enjoy the benefits of material goods without letting them control one's life. Mindful purchasing decisions play a crucial role in this balance, where individuals take the time to evaluate whether an item truly adds value to their lives before making a purchase. By shifting the focus from quantity to quality, people can invest in fewer, better-quality items that last longer and serve a greater purpose. This balance also involves rethinking the role of possessions in one's life, valuing experiences, relationships, and personal growth over the accumulation of things. By consciously choosing what to bring into their lives, individuals can reduce the stress and dissatisfaction that often accompany consumerism while still enjoying the practical and aesthetic benefits of material goods.

Through mindful consumption and a focus on quality, individuals can strike a balance between minimalism and consumerism, fostering a healthier relationship with material possessions and enhancing their overall quality of life.

Goal Setting

Setting SMART goals is essential for achieving both personal and professional growth. SMART goals are Specific, Measurable, Achievable, Relevant, and Time-bound, providing clarity and direction. For example, rather than setting a vague goal like "improve work performance," a SMART goal might be "increase productivity by 20% over the next three months by implementing time-blocking techniques." This goal is specific, measurable by the percentage increase, achievable through clear methods, relevant to professional development, and time-bound with a three-month deadline. By breaking larger objectives into smaller, more manageable steps, individuals can monitor their progress and stay motivated as they reach each milestone.

Self-Assessment

Self-assessment is a vital tool for ongoing personal growth and development. Methods like journaling allow individuals to reflect on their daily experiences, identify patterns, and recognize areas where they excel or need improvement. Reflection exercises, such as end-of-week reviews, can help individuals assess how effectively they balance their work and personal life. Another helpful method is conducting a personal SWOT analysis, which examines one's strengths, weaknesses, opportunities, and threats. This analysis can provide valuable insights into growth areas and inform decisions for future development. By regularly assessing their progress and identifying areas for improvement, individuals can stay on track toward achieving balance in their personal and professional lives.

These techniques empower individuals to take charge of their development, helping them create and maintain a balanced, fulfilling lifestyle while progressing toward their goals.

Family Planning and Communication

Effective family planning and communication are essential for balancing responsibilities and ensuring quality time together. Family meetings can be a regular opportunity to discuss schedules, responsibilities, and any issues that need attention, fostering an open dialogue between family members. Using shared calendars, whether physical or digital, helps everyone stay organized and aware of each other's commitments, reducing the likelihood of scheduling conflicts. Collaborative decision-making is another important aspect, where family members can work together to prioritize tasks and activities, ensuring that everyone's needs are considered and addressed. Clear and consistent communication keeps the household running smoothly and strengthens family bonds, as everyone feels heard and valued.

Creating Quality Family Time

Balancing the demands of daily life with meaningful family time requires intentional effort. Activities such as family dinners, where everyone gathers to share a meal and engage in conversation, help strengthen connections and provide a routine opportunity for bonding. Game nights and outdoor activities, like hiking or picnics, offer fun and engaging ways to spend time together while encouraging teamwork and communication. These activities promote relaxation and enjoyment, helping to counteract the stress of daily responsibilities. The benefits of spending quality time as a family extend beyond the present moment, as they contribute to long-term emotional well-being and deeper relationships between family members.

By planning together and intentionally creating space for quality time, families can find a balance that supports both personal growth and strong relationships, leading to a more harmonious and fulfilling family life.

Real-World Examples and Case Studies

Success Stories of Individuals Balancing Work and Life

Achieving a harmonious balance between work and personal life can be challenging, but many individuals have successfully navigated this journey, learning valuable lessons along the way. One such example is *John*, a high-level executive in the tech industry. For years, John struggled with long hours, constant travel, and the stress of leading a global team. Despite his professional success, his personal life suffered as he felt increasingly disconnected from his family. Realizing that a change was needed, John turned to time management techniques, such as blocking and setting clear boundaries between work and personal time. He began implementing "no-work weekends" and a daily "shutdown ritual," allowing him to focus entirely on his family in the evenings. Although the transition was difficult, John now reports a significant improvement in his quality of life, attributing his success to setting firm boundaries and recognizing the need for time to recharge.

Another compelling case is *Emily*, a freelance graphic designer and mother of two young children. Like many parents juggling work and family, Emily was overwhelmed with the constant demands of her clients and her role at home. She adopted a flexible work schedule, blocking time during her children's school hours for focused, deep work and reserving afternoons and evenings for family activities. By incorporating mindfulness practices and communicating her availability to clients, Emily has created a healthy balance that enables her to be productive and present in her family life. Her story highlights the importance of adaptability and transparency in achieving work-life balance.

Minimalist Lifestyles

Minimalism, which focuses on the essentials and reduces excess, has become a popular approach for individuals and families seeking simplicity and clarity in their lives. *The Thompson family* is a prime example of the benefits of minimalist living. After years of feeling burdened by the constant accumulation of material possessions and the hectic pace of their careers, the Thompsons consciously downsized their home. They reduced their belongings to only what was necessary. By simplifying their environment and removing distractions, they could focus on what mattered most: quality family time, health, and personal growth. Their journey into minimalism has led to a renewed sense of purpose and fulfillment, as they now spend more time together, travel more frequently, and experience less financial strain.

Similarly, *Lisa*, a writer and creative professional, embraced a minimalist lifestyle after feeling overwhelmed by the constant pursuit of more projects, more income, and more possessions. She realized that her quest for success had come at the expense of her mental well-being. By reducing her work commitments and simplifying her living space, Lisa could focus on her passion for writing, which the clutter of her busy life had overshadowed. Her minimalist approach extended beyond material possessions; she began focusing on meaningful relationships and personal growth, resulting in greater peace and fulfillment.

Both stories highlight the transformative impact of adopting a minimalist lifestyle, particularly in terms of material possessions and one's approach to life. By prioritizing quality over quantity, these individuals have found greater contentment and clarity, demonstrating that sometimes, less truly is more.

Learning from Challenges

Overcoming Burnout

Burnout has become a widespread issue in today's fast-paced world, where constant pressure to perform in professional and personal realms can lead to physical and emotional exhaustion. Common signs of burnout include chronic fatigue, detachment from work or personal responsibilities, decreased productivity, and feelings of helplessness or hopelessness. Recognizing these early signs is crucial to taking proactive steps toward recovery.

Sarah's story is a powerful example of overcoming burnout. As a marketing executive, Sarah thrived on the excitement of launching new campaigns and working long hours to meet tight deadlines. However, after years of relentless pressure, Sarah began to feel increasingly disconnected from her work. She lost her enthusiasm, struggled to focus, and felt emotionally drained. Realizing she could no longer continue at this pace, Sarah took a leave of absence to focus on her mental and physical health. During this period, she explored mindfulness practices, including meditation and journaling, which helped her reconnect with her core values and priorities. Slowly, she reintegrated into her work life, but with a new approach: setting firm boundaries, taking regular breaks, and focusing on sustainable productivity rather than constant hustle. Sarah's journey illustrates that recovering from burnout requires a holistic approach, combining self-awareness, rest, and gradual lifestyle changes.

Another personal recovery story comes from *Michael*, a software developer who faced burnout after years of juggling multiple freelance projects. Michael loved his work but found that his inability to say "no" to new opportunities caused him to work late at night and weekends, sacrificing sleep and personal time. His burnout manifested in physical symptoms like frequent headaches and emotional numbness. Recognizing these signs, Michael sought therapy and developed a structured work schedule with built-in rest periods. He also became more selective about his accepted projects, learning that quality work comes from a well-rested, balanced mind. His recovery journey serves as a poignant reminder that establishing boundaries and prioritizing self-care are crucial for achieving long-term success and maintaining overall well-being.

Navigating Consumer Pressures

Consumer culture often encourages the pursuit of more material goods, status symbols, and financial success. However, the pressure to keep up with societal expectations can lead to dissatisfaction and a sense of never having enough. Many individuals have resisted these pressures, adopting strategies to redefine success and find contentment in simpler, more intentional living.

Take *Jessica* and *David*, a couple who found themselves trapped in a cycle of consumerism. They were constantly upgrading their gadgets, buying new clothes, and keeping up with the latest trends, all while feeling increasingly unfulfilled. After a financial setback that forced them to reassess their spending habits, they realized how much of their consumption was driven by external pressures rather than genuine needs or desires. They decided to take a different approach, embracing minimalism and focusing on experiences rather than possessions. Jessica and David discovered deeper satisfaction by setting financial goals, curbing impulse buying, and prioritizing time spent with loved ones. Their journey highlights the importance of shifting focus from acquiring things to nurturing relationships and experiences that truly matter.

Similarly, *Tom*, a young professional in the fashion industry, felt constant pressure to keep up with trends and always present himself in the latest designer clothing. This led him to overspend and feel anxious about his image. After reflecting on the unsustainable nature of this lifestyle, Tom chose to adopt a capsule wardrobe—a small, curated collection of versatile, high-quality clothing that fit his style. This decision saved him money and reduced the stress of constantly trying to keep up with trends. Tom's story illustrates how stepping away from consumer culture can lead to greater self-confidence and clarity.

These stories demonstrate that navigating consumer pressures requires a combination of self-awareness, intentionality, and the courage to define success on one's terms. Whether overcoming the need for constant consumption or redefining what brings happiness, finding balance can lead to lasting contentment.

Future Trends and Opportunities

Technology and Personal Development

As technology evolves, its role in personal development has become increasingly significant, presenting both opportunities and challenges. Two emerging trends—digital wellness and online learning—illustrate how individuals can harness technology to enhance their well-being and growth while navigating the potential downsides of constant connectivity.

Digital Wellness

Maintaining a healthy relationship with technology is more critical than ever in a world where smartphones, tablets, and laptops are ubiquitous. Digital wellness has emerged as a growing trend, encouraging individuals to use technology mindfully and in ways that enhance their overall well-being. Digital wellness promotes a balanced approach to technology use, ensuring that it serves as a tool for productivity and connection rather than a source of distraction or stress.

One aspect of digital wellness is the practice of digital detox, where individuals intentionally take breaks from their devices to focus on real-world experiences, relationships, and self-care. Apps such as *Moment*, *Forest*, and *Stay Focused* help users limit screen time by setting timers or blocking distracting apps. These tools empower individuals to reclaim their time and attention, thereby reducing the negative effects of overuse, including anxiety, sleep disruption, and reduced productivity.

Quality verses Quantity: Is There a Middle Way?

The growing awareness of digital wellness has also sparked a movement toward creating tech-free zones or hours in households, allowing family members to engage in meaningful, device-free interactions.

Moreover, technology can foster mindfulness and well-being through apps like Headspace and Calm, which offer guided meditation, relaxation techniques, and tools for enhancing mental health. By incorporating these practices into their daily routines, individuals can cultivate a more balanced relationship with technology, utilizing it to support rather than hinder personal growth.

Online Learning and Personal Growth

The rise of online learning platforms has revolutionized how individuals access education, offering unprecedented opportunities for personal growth. Platforms like *Coursera*, *Udemy*, and *LinkedIn Learning* provide a vast array of courses in fields ranging from data science to creative writing, allowing learners to acquire new skills, expand their knowledge, and even earn certifications from the comfort of their own homes. This accessibility has democratized education, allowing anyone with an internet connection to pursue personal or professional development.

Maria, a mid-career professional, illustrates the potential of online learning. After spending over a decade in a stagnant role, she needed to enhance her skills but lacked the time to enroll in traditional courses. Through online platforms, Maria could take project management and digital marketing courses, earning certifications that ultimately allowed her to pivot herself into a new and more fulfilling career. Her experience demonstrates the versatility and convenience of online learning, which can be tailored to fit a variety of schedules and needs.

Online learning also fosters a culture of lifelong learning, encouraging individuals to seek new knowledge and improve their skills continually. This has become especially relevant in today's rapidly changing job market, where staying up-to-date with the latest technologies and trends is essential. The availability of niche courses, from technical skills like coding to personal development topics such as emotional intelligence, empowers individuals to take control of their learning journeys. These platforms provide the knowledge and the motivation to grow and adapt continuously, enhancing both personal satisfaction and career success.

As digital wellness and online learning evolve, individuals are finding innovative ways to leverage technology for self-improvement. The future of personal development lies in the mindful integration of these trends, ensuring that technology serves as a bridge to greater well-being and lifelong growth, rather than an obstacle.

Sustainable Living

Eco-Friendly Lifestyle Choices

As the world becomes more aware of our planet's environmental challenges, the trend toward sustainable living has gained momentum. Individuals increasingly seek ways to reduce their ecological footprint and make conscious decisions that positively impact the environment and their quality of life. Sustainable living emphasizes the balance between quality and quantity, encouraging thoughtful consumption and the adoption of eco-friendly practices.

One of the most accessible ways to embrace sustainability is through waste reduction. Simple changes such as reducing single-use plastics, recycling, and composting can significantly lower household waste. Adopting a minimalist approach to possessions—choosing quality, durable items over fast fashion or disposable goods—can reduce consumption and waste. This shift toward fewer, more meaningful purchases benefits the environment and enhances the individual's relationship with material goods, fostering a sense of satisfaction and intentionality.

Conserving energy is another key element of sustainable living. Energy-efficient appliances, LED lighting, and mindful use of heating and cooling systems are practical steps that reduce energy consumption and lower utility bills. Incorporating renewable energy sources, such as solar panels, into homes is becoming more affordable and accessible, offering a long-term solution to reducing reliance on fossil fuels.

Supporting sustainable brands is an increasingly important aspect of eco-conscious living. By choosing companies that prioritize ethical sourcing, fair labor practices, and environmentally friendly production methods, individuals can align their consumption habits with their values. Brands that focus on sustainable agriculture, zero-waste packaging, or cruelty-free practices enable consumers to make impactful choices, contributing to a more sustainable global economy.

The benefits of sustainable living extend beyond environmental impact. They enrich personal lives by encouraging simplicity, mindfulness, and a greater connection to nature. As individuals shift their focus from quantity to quality in their consumption habits, they often find greater contentment and purpose in their daily lives.

Community and Social Impact

Sustainability encompasses personal lifestyle choices and how individuals interact with and contribute to their communities. By engaging in activities that promote social good, individuals can make a meaningful impact on both a local and global scale. Community involvement enhances the quality of life for others and fosters a sense of belonging and purpose in the individual.

One powerful way to contribute is through volunteerism. Whether participating in neighborhood clean-ups, mentoring at-risk youth, or volunteering at food banks, individuals can directly improve the lives of those around them while fostering a sense of community. For example, Kate, a working professional, began volunteering at a local animal shelter in her free time. This helped her connect with her community and gave her a sense of fulfillment that her job alone didn't offer. Kate's story illustrates how small acts of service can have a profound impact on personal satisfaction and social well-being.

Social entrepreneurship is another avenue for making a positive impact. Entrepreneurs like *Tom*, who founded a company that produces eco-friendly cleaning products, use their businesses to address social and environmental challenges. By aligning profit with purpose, social entrepreneurs create opportunities for consumers to support causes they believe in while providing practical solutions to everyday problems. Tom's company, for example, uses biodegradable packaging and donates a portion of its profits to environmental conservation efforts, demonstrating how businesses can lead the way in sustainability and social responsibility.

Community-building activities, such as organizing local events or supporting small businesses, also strengthen the social fabric. During the COVID-19 pandemic, many individuals turned to community groups and grassroots efforts to help one another in times of crisis. Whether through organizing mutual aid networks or simply checking in on neighbors, these actions build community resilience and solidarity.

By contributing to their communities and embracing social responsibility, individuals not only enhance the quality of life for those around them but also find a more profound sense of purpose and fulfillment. Sustainable living is not just about reducing waste or conserving energy; it's about creating a more connected, compassionate world where individuals and communities thrive.

Reflection on Personal Development and Lifestyle Choices

Throughout this chapter, we have explored the intricate balance between quality and quantity in personal development and lifestyle choices. Whether through achieving work-life harmony, adopting minimalist practices, or embracing sustainable living, the common theme is intentionality. By being mindful of how we allocate our time, energy, and resources, we can shape a life that is not only productive but also fulfilling.

We've discussed real-world examples of individuals who have successfully navigated these challenges, demonstrating that balance is achievable. Whether overcoming burnout or resisting the pressures of consumerism, their stories remind us that quality, when prioritized, leads to more meaningful experiences and deeper satisfaction. We also examined future trends, such as digital wellness and online learning, which present new growth opportunities, as well as the importance of contributing to our communities through sustainable living and social impact. The key takeaway is that focusing on quality over quantity leads to a richer, more purposeful life.

Encouragement for Personal Growth

As you reflect on the concepts in this chapter, consider how you can apply these ideas to your own life. Achieving balance is not a one-time decision but an ongoing journey. It requires self-awareness, adaptability, and the willingness to grow. The practices discussed—whether mindful tech use, continuous learning, or sustainable living—are tools that can guide you toward a more intentional and balanced existence.

Remember that personal growth is a continuous process. Small, incremental changes can compound over time, leading to significant transformations. By being mindful of the choices you make each day, you can create a life that reflects your values and priorities. Whether it's through simplifying your surroundings, deepening your relationships, or engaging in purposeful work, each step toward balance is a step toward a more fulfilling life.

Take this opportunity to commit to your journey of self-improvement and intentional living. The balance between quality and quantity may seem elusive sometimes, but it is within reach with reflection and consistent effort. Embrace the practices that resonate with you and let them guide you toward a productive and enriching life.

Quality verses Quantity: Is There a Middle Way?

The Middle Way

Strategies for Achieving Balance

Finding balance in life and work often requires intentional effort and the application of proven strategies. This chapter examines practical tools and methods that can help individuals and organizations strike a balance between quality and quantity. These strategies emphasize continuous improvement, strategic alignment, and effective time management — essential elements for maintaining balance in a fast-paced world.

Kaizen (Continuous Improvement)

The Japanese concept of *Kaizen*, meaning "change for the better" or "continuous improvement," is a philosophy that encourages making small, incremental changes to enhance efficiency and quality. Rather than seeking drastic, immediate transformation, Kaizen focuses on gradual, consistent improvements that, over time, lead to significant results. Initially developed in the context of manufacturing, Kaizen has since been applied to various industries and personal development efforts.

A key aspect of Kaizen is the involvement of everyone, from leadership to frontline workers, in identifying areas for improvement. For example, in a workplace setting, Kaizen events or workshops are organized to analyze processes, brainstorm improvements, and implement actionable changes. One company that has successfully adopted this method is *Toyota*, whose production system incorporates Kaizen principles. Toyota has maintained its reputation for high-quality production and innovation by continually refining processes and empowering employees to contribute ideas.

On an individual level, Kaizen can be applied to personal goals. For instance, someone seeking to improve their health may begin by making small changes to their diet or exercise routine, such as adding a short walk to their daily schedule or reducing sugar intake. When consistently practiced, these minor adjustments lead to lasting improvements over time. The beauty of Kaizen lies in its simplicity and accessibility—anyone can adopt this method to enhance their life, whether in professional or personal contexts.

Balanced Scorecards

The balanced scorecard is a valuable strategic tool for organizations seeking a balance between long-term vision and day-to-day operations. Developed by Robert Kaplan and David Norton, it enables companies to align their activities with their broader vision and strategy. This is achieved by focusing on four key perspectives: financial, customer, internal processes, and learning and growth.

The balanced scorecard helps organizations move beyond purely financial metrics by integrating non-financial indicators, such as customer satisfaction and employee development. This holistic approach enables businesses to comprehensively understand their performance and progress toward strategic goals. For example, a company may set objectives related to customer loyalty, operational efficiency, and employee training, all while tracking traditional financial metrics. By doing so, the organization ensures that its efforts are balanced and aligned with its overall mission.

In addition to strategic planning, the balanced scorecard improves internal and external communications. It provides a clear framework for managers and employees to understand how their work contributes to the company's success. Externally, it helps communicate the organization's strategic priorities to stakeholders, including investors, customers, and partners.

Time Management Techniques

Achieving balance requires effective time management. Time is a finite resource that, when used wisely, can significantly enhance productivity and personal fulfillment. Several time management techniques have proven highly effective in helping individuals prioritize tasks and manage their workloads.

Quality verses Quantity: Is There a Middle Way?

One such technique is the *Eisenhower Matrix*, named after President Dwight D. Eisenhower, who was known for his exceptional productivity. The matrix divides tasks into four categories based on urgency and importance:

1. Urgent and important
2. Important but not urgent
3. Urgent but not important
4. Neither urgent nor important

By categorizing tasks, individuals can focus on what truly matters and avoid getting caught up in activities that offer little value. The matrix helps clarify priorities, allowing people to make more informed decisions about allocating their time.

Another popular method is *time blocking*, where specific periods are set aside for focused work on particular tasks. By scheduling tasks into blocks of time, individuals can limit distractions and ensure steady progress on their most important activities. This method is beneficial for those who struggle with multitasking or have difficulty concentrating for extended periods.

The *Pomodoro Technique* provides a time management approach that divides work into intervals, typically 25 minutes long, followed by brief breaks. This method harnesses the power of short bursts of focused work, enabling individuals to maintain their energy and focus throughout the day. The technique's effectiveness stems from its simplicity and the inherent reward of taking a break, which can boost motivation and prevent burnout.

By adopting one or more of these time management techniques, individuals can find a greater balance between their responsibilities and personal time, ensuring they remain productive without feeling overwhelmed.

Role of Leadership and Organizational Culture

Leadership is pivotal in striking the right balance between quality and quantity within an organization. The tone set by leaders and the organizational culture they foster can drive sustainable success or lead to imbalances that impact productivity and morale. Two key aspects of leadership—vision and communication, as well as empowerment and engagement—are crucial for achieving this balance.

Vision and Communication

A clear and compelling vision is the foundation for successful organizations. When leaders articulate a vision emphasizing high-quality standards and effective productivity, they provide a roadmap for the organization. However, having a vision alone is not enough—it must be effectively communicated across all levels of the organization.

Consider the example of *Apple*, where leaders have consistently communicated a vision that prioritizes innovation without compromising quality. By setting high expectations for product development while prioritizing customer satisfaction, Apple has successfully balanced the pursuit of cutting-edge technology with the need for mass production. This balance is achieved through transparent communication from leadership, ensuring that everyone within the organization understands the overarching goals and their role in achieving them.

Leaders who communicate inspire confidence in their team and clarify how to achieve the organization's vision. By regularly discussing objectives, progress, and challenges, leaders can ensure alignment between individual efforts and the broader organizational strategy. Effective communication also fosters a culture of openness, where employees feel empowered to ask questions, offer feedback, and share ideas—ultimately contributing to the organization's ability to strike a balance between quality and quantity.

Empowerment and Engagement

Empowering employees is crucial for creating an environment where quality and productivity flourish. When employees are given the autonomy to make decisions, contribute ideas, and take ownership of their work, they become more engaged and invested in the outcomes.

Quality verses Quantity: Is There a Middle Way?

Empowered employees are more likely to deliver high-quality work, as they feel responsible and take pride in their contributions.

Google is a prime example of how leadership can promote empowerment and engagement. By providing employees with flexible work arrangements and opportunities to work on projects that interest them, Google has fostered a culture where employees are motivated to perform at their best. This sense of ownership enhances creativity and innovation, resulting in higher-quality output.

Leadership practices that promote empowerment often include offering opportunities for professional development, encouraging collaboration, and recognizing individual contributions. *Southwest Airlines* is another organization that exemplifies the power of employee engagement. By empowering frontline employees, such as flight attendants and customer service representatives, to make real-time decisions, Southwest ensures that customer needs are met quickly and efficiently. This level of trust and empowerment has contributed to the company's reputation for exceptional customer service and operational efficiency.

Engaged employees are also more likely to remain committed to their work and the organization's mission, which helps maintain consistent levels of productivity and quality. Leaders who actively engage with their teams, listen to their concerns, and involve them in decision-making create an environment where employees feel valued. This improves morale and drives a collective commitment to the organization's success.

Practical Applications and Tools

Techniques for Individuals

Achieving a balance between quality and quantity in personal and professional life requires practical tools and techniques. By setting clear goals, prioritizing tasks, and engaging in regular self-reflection, individuals can focus their time and energy on what truly matters while remaining flexible enough to adapt when necessary.

Goal Setting and Prioritization

Setting clear, achievable goals is foundational in striking a balance between quality and quantity. Without a clear direction, it's easy to become overwhelmed by competing tasks, resulting in diminished focus and inconsistent results. Practical goal setting provides a roadmap that allows individuals to prioritize their efforts and allocate resources toward activities that align with their values and objectives.

One widely used framework for goal setting is the *SMART* goals method, which stands for Specific, Measurable, Achievable, Relevant, and Time-bound. By defining goals with these criteria in mind, individuals ensure that their goals are both clear and actionable, making them trackable. For example, rather than setting a vague goal like "improve work-life balance," a SMART goal might be "reduce work hours by 10% over the next two months by delegating non-essential tasks and limiting overtime." This goal is specific, measurable, and time-bound, providing the individual with a clear target and a means to measure progress.

Prioritization is just as critical as goal setting. The *Eisenhower Matrix*, previously discussed, is one tool that can help individuals categorize their tasks based on urgency and importance. Individuals can avoid distractions and manage their time more effectively by focusing on important and urgent tasks. Prioritizing also allows for a better balance between quality and quantity, ensuring that time and energy are invested in high-impact activities without neglecting other important areas of life.

Self-Reflection and Adaptation

Self-reflection is a crucial practice for individuals seeking to maintain balance. By regularly evaluating progress and reassessing priorities, individuals can make informed decisions about where to direct their efforts. One effective self-reflection technique is journaling, which allows individuals to document their thoughts, goals, and progress over time. Writing in a journal provides a space for introspection, helping individuals identify patterns of behavior, areas for improvement, and achievements.

Regular check-ins are another valuable tool for self-reflection. Depending on the individual's needs, these sessions can be scheduled on a weekly, monthly, or quarterly basis. During these check-ins, individuals can ask themselves, "Am I on track with my goals?" "What adjustments do I need to make?" and "How do I feel about the quality of my work and personal life?" These moments of reflection can reveal whether goals need to be adjusted or new strategies are required to maintain balance.

Adaptability is key to sustaining balance in an ever-changing environment. Life is unpredictable; rigid adherence to a plan may lead to frustration when unexpected challenges arise. Individuals can adjust their goals, priorities, and strategies as needed by cultivating a mindset that embraces change, thereby ensuring they continue to move forward. Being adaptable means recognizing when something isn't working and having the flexibility to pivot, whether by delegating tasks, revisiting time management techniques, or even reevaluating long-term goals.

Self-reflection and adaptation are not one-time exercises but ongoing processes that support continuous growth and balance. By regularly assessing their progress and being open to change, individuals can maintain focus on both quality and quantity, ensuring they lead balanced and fulfilling lives.

Techniques for Organizations

Balancing quality and quantity in an organizational context requires strategic planning, clear metrics, and a commitment to continuous improvement. This section examines how organizations can utilize tools such as balanced scorecards and Lean principles to optimize processes, maintain quality, and enhance productivity.

Balanced Scorecards and Performance Metrics

The balanced scorecard, introduced earlier, is a strategic tool that helps organizations align their day-to-day activities with their broader vision. By incorporating performance metrics across financial, customer, internal processes, and learning and growth perspectives, the balanced scorecard provides a comprehensive view of how well an organization achieves its goals. When used effectively, it enables organizations to monitor progress in real-time and adjust as needed to strike a balance between quality and quantity.

One company that has successfully implemented the balanced scorecard is *Hilton Hotels*. Faced with maintaining exceptional customer service while expanding its global presence, Hilton used the balanced scorecard to track customer satisfaction, employee training, and financial performance. By focusing on various metrics, Hilton could monitor how its growth strategies impacted service quality, ensuring that quantity (expansion) did not come at the expense of quality (customer satisfaction). This approach allowed Hilton to scale its operations while preserving its reputation for top-tier service.

Performance metrics play a critical role in maintaining balance. For example, *Amazon* uses data-driven performance metrics to ensure its operations meet efficiency and customer satisfaction goals. Amazon has maintained a high volume of orders without compromising service or product standards by tracking key performance indicators (KPIs) such as delivery times, product quality, and employee performance. The metrics integration ensures that every aspect of the business is monitored, allowing for real-time adjustments when necessary.

Process Optimization and Lean Principles

Organizations must continually optimize their processes to strike a balance between quality and quantity. Lean principles, originating in manufacturing, provide a framework for reducing waste and improving efficiency while maintaining high quality. Lean thinking emphasizes delivering value to the customer by identifying and eliminating activities that do not contribute to the end product or service.

One of the core Lean principles is the concept of *Kaizen* or continuous improvement. Organizations can create a culture of constant innovation by engaging employees at all levels to identify inefficiencies and suggest improvements. *Toyota*, a pioneer in Lean manufacturing, uses Kaizen as a foundational practice in its Toyota Production System. Employees on the production line are encouraged to identify areas for improvement, which has led to significant waste reductions and quality improvements over time.

Lean tools, such as Value Stream Mapping, enable organizations to visually map out each step in a process, identifying where waste occurs and where improvements can be made. For instance, in the healthcare industry, Lean principles have been applied to streamline patient care processes, reduce waiting times, and enhance overall patient outcomes. Hospitals that implement Lean methodologies often see a decrease in inefficiencies, including redundant paperwork and unnecessary steps in treatment protocols, which improves both the quality of care and the efficiency of the operation.

Another powerful Lean tool is 5S, which stands for Sort, Set in Order, Shine, Standardize, and Sustain. This method helps organizations create more organized and efficient workplaces. For instance, 5S has been utilized in manufacturing to organize workspaces, reduce the time spent searching for tools or materials, and create a cleaner and safer work environment. By applying 5S, companies such as Boeing have improved production efficiency without compromising quality.

Lean principles can be applied across various industries, including manufacturing, healthcare, logistics, and service-based businesses. By optimizing processes through the elimination of waste, organizations can strike a balance between delivering high-quality products and services while maintaining the capacity to scale.

Real-World Examples

Case Studies of Successful Balancing Acts

Balancing quality and quantity is not just a theoretical concept but has been successfully implemented by some of the world's leading organizations. By studying these companies, we can gain insights into how they have managed to maintain high standards while scaling operations and achieving growth.

Google

Google is often cited as a leading example of how innovation and efficiency coexist. One key strategy Google employs to foster creativity without sacrificing operational efficiency is its *20%-time policy*. This policy enables employees to dedicate 20% of their work time to projects they are passionate about, even if those projects are not directly related to their primary responsibilities.

This approach has led to the development of some of Google's most successful products, including Gmail and Google News. By allowing employees to explore their creative ideas, Google fosters continuous innovation. However, this freedom is balanced with a focus on efficiency. The company's core operations—such as its search engine and cloud services—are tightly managed using data-driven metrics and performance indicators to ensure these essential services run smoothly and efficiently.

Google's balancing act involves creating a structure that supports both exploration and disciplined execution. The 20%-time policy is a testament to the company's belief that creativity flourishes when employees are given space to innovate. It is complemented by strong processes and rigorous management of its core business functions. This combination allows Google to maintain its leadership in the tech industry while continuing to innovate.

Toyota

Toyota is another prime example of a company that has successfully balanced quality and quantity by applying *Lean principles*. The Toyota Production System (TPS) is renowned for producing high-quality vehicles at scale, focusing on efficiency, waste reduction, and continuous improvement.

One key component of Toyota's success is its use of *Kaizen*, a philosophy of continuous improvement. Employees at all levels are encouraged to identify areas for improvement, no matter how small, which has led to ongoing enhancements in production processes. This focus on incremental changes ensures that Toyota maintains high-quality standards while constantly seeking improvements in efficiency.

Toyota's ability to balance large-scale production with quality is also supported by its *Just-in-Time* manufacturing process. By producing vehicles and parts only when needed, Toyota minimizes waste and reduces inventory costs, allowing the company to operate more efficiently. This process, combined with Kaizen, enables Toyota to meet high production demands while maintaining the quality of its vehicles.

The result is a company that leads in production volume and consistently ranks high in customer satisfaction and product reliability. Toyota's Lean principles model how organizations can scale efficiently while maintaining a commitment to quality.

Southwest Airlines

Southwest Airlines has long been admired for striking a balance between operational efficiency and exceptional customer service. Its unique business model, which focuses on low-cost fares and streamlined operations, has allowed Southwest to become one of the most profitable airlines in the industry while maintaining a loyal customer base.

One key element of Southwest's success is its emphasis on *employee empowerment and engagement*. The company believes that happy employees lead to happy customers, and this philosophy is reflected in its corporate culture. Southwest encourages employees to take the initiative and make decisions that enhance the customer experience, whether that involves resolving issues promptly or adding a personal touch to interactions.

Southwest's operational efficiency is driven by using a single aircraft type, the Boeing 737, across its entire fleet. This simplifies maintenance and training, allowing the airline to minimize costs and turn planes around quickly between flights. At the same time, the company places a high value on customer service, with a no-frills approach that still prioritizes passenger comfort and satisfaction. By balancing these two priorities, Southwest has developed a business model that delivers both efficiency and quality, distinguishing itself in an industry characterized by tight margins and intense competition.

Southwest's success demonstrates that operational excellence can be achieved while maintaining a strong focus on customer satisfaction. The company's business model, corporate culture, and strategic decisions are all balanced in terms of both quantity (in terms of flights and passengers served) and quality (in terms of customer experience).

Learning from Failures

Case Studies of Imbalance

While some companies have successfully balanced quality and quantity, others have faced significant challenges when one was prioritized at the expense of the other. Examining failures can provide valuable lessons about the risks of compromising quality for the sake of speed or cost efficiency. Two prominent examples are the Volkswagen emissions scandal and the Boeing 737 Max crisis, which underscore the consequences of failing to maintain this balance.

Volkswagen Emissions Scandal

The Volkswagen emissions scandal, which erupted in 2015, serves as a cautionary tale of how prioritizing production and market share over ethical practices and quality can have devastating consequences. Volkswagen, once a symbol of German engineering excellence, found itself embroiled in a massive corporate scandal when it was revealed that the company had intentionally installed software in its diesel vehicles to cheat emissions tests.

The root of the scandal lies in Volkswagen's ambition to become the world's largest automaker. In its drive to dominate the global market, the company faced pressure to meet stringent emissions standards while continuing to produce vehicles that appealed to consumers seeking both performance and environmental friendliness. Rather than invest in the necessary technology to meet these standards, Volkswagen opted for a shortcut: software that would activate emissions controls only during testing, allowing the vehicles to emit far higher levels of pollutants during everyday driving.

Quality verses Quantity: Is There a Middle Way?

The fallout from the scandal was severe. Volkswagen faced billions of dollars in fines, legal settlements, and recall costs, in addition to the loss of consumer trust and a tarnished brand reputation. The company's stock price plummeted, and senior executives resigned or were dismissed. Beyond the financial penalties, the scandal served as a stark reminder of the dangers of compromising quality and ethical standards for short-term gains.

The lessons from Volkswagen's failure are clear: when companies prioritize quantity—whether in terms of production, market share, or profits—over quality, the long-term consequences can be catastrophic. For Volkswagen, the decision to cut corners undermined the integrity of its product and had a lasting impact on its brand, which will take years to recover fully. The scandal serves as a reminder that maintaining a balance between quality, ethics, and quantity is crucial for sustained success.

Boeing 737 Max

Another high-profile example of a failure to balance quality and quantity occurred with Boeing and its 737 Max aircraft. In the wake of two tragic crashes in 2018 and 2019 that resulted in the loss of 346 lives, investigations revealed that Boeing had rushed the development and production of the 737 Max to compete with its European rival, Airbus. The desire to bring the new aircraft to market quickly led to compromises in safety and quality control.

At the heart of the issue was Boeing's decision to implement new software, the Maneuvering Characteristics Augmentation System (MCAS), to address the 737 Max's tendency to pitch upward. However, the company failed to adequately inform pilots about the system. It was later discovered that Boeing had not required extensive pilot retraining to avoid delays and additional airline costs. Furthermore, critical safety issues with the MCAS system were either overlooked or not communicated effectively.

The crashes and subsequent grounding of the 737 Max fleet had far-reaching consequences for Boeing. The company faced intense scrutiny from regulators, legal action from victims' families, and severe damage to its reputation. Boeing's production lines were disrupted, and the financial impact was immense, with the company incurring billions of dollars in losses due to grounded planes, compensation to airlines, and lost orders.

The Boeing 737 Max crisis highlights the dangers of prioritizing production speed and cost efficiency over safety and quality control. The rush to bring a product to market, combined with inadequate safety oversight, led to tragic consequences. Boeing's experience serves as a reminder that in industries where safety is paramount, the pressure to deliver quickly must be balanced with rigorous quality checks and a commitment to safety standards.

The lessons from Boeing's failure underscore the importance of maintaining a culture that prioritizes quality and safety, especially when the stakes are high. Companies that focus too heavily on speed and cost-cutting risk not only financial losses but also irreparable damage to their reputation and, in some cases, the safety of their customers.

Challenges and Opportunities

Common Obstacles in Striving for Balance

Achieving a balance between quality and quantity often presents a range of challenges for both individuals and organizations. Limited resources and resistance to change are two of the most common obstacles in this pursuit. However, understanding these challenges also opens the door to opportunities for growth and improvement.

Resource Constraints

One of the most significant challenges in balancing quality and quantity is the constraint of resources—whether budget, time, or workforce. Organizations and individuals often face pressure to produce more with less, leading to difficult trade-offs between maintaining high standards and meeting productivity demands.

Resource constraints may be manifested in tight budgets for businesses, requiring difficult decisions about where to allocate funds. When resources are stretched thin, it can be tempting to prioritize output over quality. For example, a company may cut costs by reducing staff, which can result in increased workloads and a potential for errors or diminished quality. Similarly, when budgets are restricted, investments in quality improvements or new technologies may be delayed or reduced in scope.

Time constraints also play a critical role in the struggle for balance. In fast-paced industries, the pressure to meet tight deadlines can lead to rushed work, compromising quality. Individuals, too, face the challenge of balancing the demands of work, family, and personal development within the limited hours of the day. The scarcity of time often forces people to make tough decisions about prioritizing their activities. Quality can easily take a backseat to quantity without effective time management strategies.

Workforce, or the lack thereof, is another resource constraint that can hinder the pursuit of balance. When organizations are understaffed, employees are often expected to do more with less support, which can lead to burnout, a decline in morale, and a drop in productivity. In these scenarios, quality suffers as employees struggle to keep up with increasing demands.

Despite these challenges, resource constraints can also create opportunities for innovation. Limited resources often compel individuals and organizations to think creatively, finding innovative ways to enhance efficiency and productivity without compromising quality. Lean principles, for example, are designed to optimize processes even in resource-constrained environments, demonstrating that with the right mindset and strategies, it's possible to do more with less.

Resistance to Change

Another common obstacle to achieving balance is resistance to change. Change can be unsettling, especially within organizations with deeply ingrained cultures or long-standing practices. Employees may fear that new processes or tools will disrupt their workflow or make their jobs more difficult. Similarly, leaders may resist change if they believe existing methods are sufficient or are concerned about the short-term costs of implementing improvements.

Resistance to change is not limited to organizations; it also affects individuals. Whether changing a routine, adopting new time management techniques, or adjusting personal habits, people often resist change due to uncertainty or a fear of failure. This reluctance can hinder achieving balance, as old habits of prioritizing quantity over quality may persist.

Overcoming resistance to change requires a proactive approach. For organizations, fostering a culture of continuous improvement is essential. Leaders must communicate the benefits of change, highlighting how new techniques can enhance productivity and quality. Involving employees in the change process through workshops, feedback sessions, or collaborative planning can also help ease fears and encourage buy-in. By empowering employees to take ownership of improvements, organizations can foster a culture that embraces change as a means to achieve better results.

Self-awareness and flexibility are crucial to overcoming resistance on an individual level. Developing a growth mindset—where challenges are viewed as opportunities for learning—can help individuals navigate change more effectively. Regular self-reflection and goal setting can also provide direction and motivation, enabling individuals to stay focused on the benefits of adopting new practices that promote balance.

While resistance to change is a natural response, it also presents an opportunity for growth. When organizations and individuals learn to embrace change and adapt, they open the door to continuous improvement, achieving a lasting balance between quality and quantity.

Strategies for Overcoming Obstacles

Navigating Challenges with Effective Approaches

When faced with obstacles in balancing quality and quantity, organizations and individuals must employ strategic methods to overcome these challenges. Two key strategies for overcoming common barriers are applying change management principles and embracing innovation and adaptability.

Change Management

Change management is a structured approach to transitioning individuals, teams, or entire organizations from their current state to a desired future state. Effective change management ensures smooth, well-planned, and sustainable transitions, whether introducing new processes, implementing technological upgrades, or shifting an organization's culture.

One widely used model is *Kotter's 8-Step Process for Leading Change*, which outlines key steps for successful change management. The process begins with creating a sense of urgency for change, building a guiding coalition, forming a strategic vision, and communicating that vision clearly throughout the organization. The latter step involves empowering employees to take action, generating short-term wins to maintain momentum, consolidating gains, and anchoring new approaches in the organizational culture.

A successful example of change management in practice is the transformation of *General Electric (GE)* under the leadership of CEO Jack Welch in the 1980s. Welch implemented sweeping changes focused on efficiency, accountability, and innovation, transforming GE into a highly profitable and streamlined organization. One of his most effective change management techniques was the introduction of *Six Sigma*, a quality management methodology focused on eliminating defects and improving processes. Through strong leadership, clear communication, and a commitment to continuous improvement, Welch navigated GE through a period of significant transition, ensuring that the company emerged more competitive and efficient.

Changing management principles can also be applied on a personal level. By recognizing the need for change, setting clear goals, and developing a plan to achieve those goals, individuals can manage transitions in their own lives, whether adopting new time management strategies, adjusting work habits, or pursuing personal growth. Self-discipline, regular reflection, and breaking down changes into manageable steps are essential for navigating personal transitions smoothly.

Innovation and Adaptation

Innovation and adapting are critical for organizations and individuals in an ever-changing environment. Embracing innovation means being open to new technologies, methodologies, and approaches that can enhance quality and efficiency. At the same time, adaptability ensures that individuals and organizations can pivot when needed, responding to market demands, technological advancements, or shifts in customer expectations.

A prime example of successful adaptation is *Netflix*, which began as a DVD rental service but transformed into a global streaming giant as technology and consumer behavior shifted. Rather than clinging to its original business model, Netflix quickly embraced the possibilities of digital streaming. It continuously adapted its platform to include personalized recommendations, original content, and international expansion. By staying ahead of the curve, Netflix has maintained its competitive edge in an increasingly crowded market.

Companies like Siemens have also demonstrated the importance of innovation and adaptation in the manufacturing sector. Siemens has successfully integrated *Industry 4.0* technologies, such as automation, data analytics, and the Internet of Things (IoT), into its operations. These innovations have enabled Siemens to optimize production processes, reduce waste, and enhance product quality. By embracing technological advancements, Siemens has remained at the forefront of its industry while striking a balance between production efficiency and high-quality outputs.

On an individual level, innovation and adaptability are essential for personal growth. The rapid pace of technological change and evolving work environments necessitate that individuals continually learn new skills, adopt new tools, and adapt their approaches. This may involve learning to use new software, developing soft skills such as emotional intelligence, or staying current with industry trends. Being adaptable allows individuals to navigate these changes smoothly, ensuring they remain competitive and relevant in both their personal and professional lives.

Organizations and individuals can turn obstacles into opportunities by embracing innovation and fostering adaptability. The ability to navigate change effectively and adopt new technologies or methods is not just a strategy for overcoming challenges; it's a pathway to continuous improvement and long-term success.

Future Trends and Opportunities

Technological Advancements

As technology evolves, it presents both challenges and opportunities for balancing quality and quantity. Two major areas of advancement—automation and artificial intelligence (AI), as well as data analytics and predictive modeling—offer the potential to optimize processes, enhance decision-making, and improve quality and efficiency.

Automation and AI

Automation and AI have rapidly become essential tools in industries ranging from manufacturing to healthcare. These technologies can revolutionize organizations' operations by reducing human error, streamlining processes, and enhancing productivity. Automation, particularly in repetitive or labor-intensive tasks, allows businesses to scale operations without compromising quality, as machines can work continuously and with greater precision than human labor.

One notable example is *robotic process automation (RPA)* in industries such as finance and customer service, where routine tasks like data entry, invoicing, and customer support queries can be handled by AI-powered systems. This frees human workers to focus on higher-value activities and reduces the risk of errors associated with manual data handling.

In manufacturing, *automated assembly lines* have long been a hallmark of efficiency. However, advancements in AI now enable machines to perform more complex tasks, such as quality control and predictive maintenance. AI systems can utilize sensors to monitor machinery in real-time, predicting potential failures before they occur and scheduling maintenance accordingly, thereby minimizing downtime and ensuring consistent product quality.

However, automation and AI also present challenges, particularly in terms of workforce displacement and the need for new skills. As machines take over more tasks, there may be fewer opportunities for manual labor, raising concerns about workers' job security. To address these challenges, organizations must invest in upskilling and reskilling programs to ensure employees can transition into new roles that complement automation, such as overseeing AI systems or focusing on creative problem-solving.

Despite these challenges, automation and AI offer significant potential for striking a balance between quality and quantity. Organizations can maintain high-quality standards while increasing output by allowing machines to handle repetitive or error-prone tasks, thereby enhancing productivity.

Data Analytics and Predictive Modeling

Data analytics and predictive modeling are another key technological advancement that is reshaping industries. These tools enable organizations to make data-driven decisions, optimize their operations, and anticipate future trends—all of which contribute to achieving a better balance between quality and quantity.

Data analytics involves collecting, analyzing, and interpreting large datasets to gain insights into business performance, customer behavior, or operational efficiency. When applied effectively, data analytics can help organizations identify areas for improvement, streamline processes, and allocate resources more efficiently. For instance, retailers can utilize data analytics to monitor inventory levels in real-time, ensuring they are neither overstocking nor understocking products. This helps reduce waste and improve customer satisfaction.

Predictive modeling, a subset of data analytics, uses historical data and statistical algorithms to forecast future events. By leveraging predictive models, organizations can anticipate customer demand, optimize supply chains, and even predict equipment malfunctions before they happen. For example, airlines use predictive modeling to optimize flight routes, fuel consumption, and maintenance schedules, improving operational efficiency and the quality of service provided to passengers.

A powerful example of data analytics in action can be found in *Amazon's* supply chain management. Amazon's algorithms can predict purchasing patterns and optimize inventory levels at warehouses worldwide by analyzing data from millions of transactions and customer interactions. This ensures that products are always in stock and delivered quickly, meeting high customer expectations for quality and efficiency.

As organizations adopt data-driven approaches, integrating data analytics and predictive modeling will become essential for maintaining a competitive edge. These tools enhance decision-making and enable organizations to anticipate challenges and opportunities, allowing for more strategic and balanced approaches to growth and development.

Sustainability and Ethical Practices

Balancing Responsibility with Profitability

In today's business environment, pursuing sustainability and ethical practices is becoming increasingly important for companies and consumers. Businesses that successfully integrate these values into their operations can enhance their reputation and strike a balance between long-term profitability and environmental and social responsibility. Sustainable business models and corporate social responsibility (CSR) are key areas where this balance is achieved.

Sustainable Business Models

As awareness of environmental issues grows, businesses are under increasing pressure to adopt sustainable practices that reduce their ecological footprint. Sustainable business models prioritize long-term environmental responsibility while ensuring profitability. These models focus on minimizing waste, conserving resources, and finding innovative ways to meet consumer demand without compromising the planet's future.

Patagonia, a clothing brand that built its business model around environmental responsibility, is leading the way in sustainability. Patagonia's commitment to sustainability is evident in its *Worn Wear* program, which encourages customers to buy used products or repair their existing gear instead of purchasing new items. The company also invests heavily in using recycled materials in its products and has pledged to donate a percentage of its profits to environmental causes. This commitment to sustainability has enhanced Patagonia's brand image and fostered a loyal customer base that values ethical consumption.

Another example is *Unilever*, which has integrated sustainability into its core business strategy through its *Sustainable Living Plan*. The company aims to reduce its environmental impact while simultaneously growing its business. Unilever has improved its profitability and environmental performance by focusing on areas such as waste reduction, water conservation, and sustainable sourcing. The company's efforts have demonstrated that sustainable practices and profitability can coexist, with consumers increasingly choosing brands that align with their values.

Sustainable business models demonstrate that environmental responsibility doesn't have to come at the cost of profitability. By investing in sustainable practices, companies can reduce costs, attract environmentally conscious customers, and establish a competitive advantage in a market that is increasingly valuing sustainability.

Corporate Social Responsibility (CSR)

Corporate social responsibility (CSR) is another vital component of balancing quality, quantity, and ethical practices. CSR initiatives allow companies to engage in activities that benefit society while enhancing their business operations. This can range from charitable giving and community engagement to ethical labor practices and environmentally friendly initiatives. Companies that successfully integrate CSR into their business models often experience enhanced brand loyalty, improved employee morale, and a stronger reputation.

One company that has effectively integrated CSR into its operations is *Ben & Jerry's*. Known for its commitment to social justice and environmental stewardship, Ben & Jerry's uses its platform to promote causes such as climate change awareness, racial equality, and fair trade. The company sources ingredients from ethical suppliers and ensures its operations align with sustainability and social justice values. By embedding CSR into its brand, Ben & Jerry's has cultivated a loyal customer base that shares its commitment to positively impacting the world.

Starbucks is another example of a company that has embraced CSR. The coffee giant's *Ethical Sourcing Program* ensures that its coffee is sourced in a way that supports farmers, protects the environment, and fosters economic stability in coffee-growing communities. Starbucks also focuses on sustainability within its supply chain, aiming to reduce waste and promote recycling through its stores. The company's CSR efforts have helped enhance its global reputation while maintaining profitability.

CSR is not just about doing good for society; it is also a powerful tool for businesses to engage with customers, employees, and stakeholders in a meaningful way. Companies that prioritize CSR create a culture of accountability and responsibility, which can lead to greater customer loyalty and long-term success.

Reflection on the Middle Way

Achieving a balance between quality and quantity is not a one-time goal but a continuous process that requires deliberate strategies, tools, and reflection. This chapter explored various approaches to navigating the challenges of striving for balance, including leveraging technological advancements and sustainability practices, as well as fostering innovation and managing change. Whether adopting Lean principles, embracing automation, or prioritizing corporate social responsibility, the key to success is finding the middle way. This path values both quality and quantity without sacrificing one for the other.

We examined real-world examples of companies like Google, Toyota, and Southwest Airlines that have successfully maintained this balance, as well as cautionary tales such as Volkswagen and Boeing, illustrating the consequences of prioritizing speed or profit over quality. These case studies reinforce the importance of aligning organizational goals with long-term sustainability and ethical practices.

Ultimately, achieving balance requires both strategic planning and a willingness to adapt to change. Whether through time management techniques, such as the Eisenhower Matrix, or the implementation of balanced scorecards in business, the practical tools outlined in this chapter provide actionable steps for individuals and organizations to maintain equilibrium.

Encouragement for Continuous Improvement

Reflecting on the strategies and examples discussed, it's essential to recognize that balance is an ongoing journey. Continuous improvement is key, whether that means making small, incremental changes in your personal life or implementing large-scale innovations in your organization. The middle way is not about perfection, but instead about consistently aligning your actions with your values.

Embrace the tools and techniques outlined in this chapter as steppingstones toward a more balanced and fulfilling life. Whether you're looking to streamline processes, adopt sustainable practices, or find more time for personal growth, the path to improvement is always open. Remember the importance of self-reflection, adaptability, and intentional living as you move forward. By making conscious decisions and prioritizing quality as much as quantity, you can create lasting changes that benefit both your personal and professional life.

Balancing quality and quantity is a lifelong endeavor, but with dedication and the right approach, achieving success in both areas is possible. Continue to improve, reflect, and strive for balance—your future self will thank you.

Challenges and Opportunities

Common Obstacles in Striving for Quality and Quantity

Resource Constraints

Resource constraints often pose significant challenges in striking a balance between quality and quantity. Whether financial, time-related, or tied to human resources, these limitations require careful planning and creative solutions to ensure that neither quality nor output suffers.

Budget Limitations

One of the most common hurdles in balancing quality and quantity is the restriction of financial resources. Organizations often find themselves in situations where budget constraints force them to make compromises. For instance, high-quality materials or advanced technology might be prohibitively expensive, leading to a focus on producing more with less —often at the cost of quality.

However, budget limitations don't necessarily mean a trade-off is inevitable. By strategically optimizing budget allocation, it is possible to maintain a balance. One approach is to prioritize investments in key areas that drive the most significant impact on quality without sacrificing necessary output. For example, a company might allocate more resources to critical stages of production, such as research and development or final quality checks, while finding cost-saving measures in less impactful areas, like packaging or marketing. Another tactic could involve renegotiating contracts with suppliers to obtain better rates on bulk materials, allowing for higher-quality input at a more affordable cost.

Real-world examples include companies that focus on lean production techniques to reduce waste and cut costs while maintaining high product quality. This approach maximizes efficiency and ensures that each dollar spent contributes to both quality and quantity.

Quality verses Quantity: Is There a Middle Way?

Time Pressures

Time is another critical factor that affects the balance between quality and quantity. In fast-paced environments, tight deadlines can make it challenging to maintain high standards while meeting production targets. This creates a dilemma: produce quickly but risk lower quality or take more time but deliver fewer products.

Effective time management techniques can alleviate some of these pressures. One method is implementing time-blocking strategies, where specific tasks are assigned set periods of focused effort. This technique allows for a structured approach, ensuring that quality isn't sacrificed in the rush to complete projects. Additionally, breaking larger projects into smaller, more manageable tasks can help teams maintain momentum while ensuring they don't lose sight of quality.

Another strategy involves using agile methodologies that allow for iterative development. By breaking down the project into phases and focusing on delivering high-quality results in each phase, organizations can ensure that quality is maintained throughout the process while still adhering to deadlines. For instance, in software development, agile teams release incremental updates, ensuring that both time and quality are respected in each release cycle.

Workforce and Skills Shortages

Limited human resources and skills gaps represent another obstacle to balancing quality and quantity. When teams are understaffed or lack the necessary expertise, it can lead to inefficiencies, slower production times, and a decrease in output quality.

Training and development are crucial to overcoming this challenge. Investing in upskilling employees bridges the skills gap, boosts morale, and increases productivity. For instance, implementing continuous learning programs enables staff to acquire new skills while staying current on industry best practices. Cross-training employees to handle multiple roles can also alleviate workforce shortages, making teams more adaptable and efficient.

Outsourcing specific tasks or automating repetitive processes can fill skill gaps or reduce the burden on limited staff. This approach enables the core team to focus on higher-quality outputs, while external support or automation handles routine tasks that do not require advanced expertise. An example of this can be seen in industries such as manufacturing, where robotic automation maintains production levels, allowing human workers to focus on areas that require precision and quality control.

By recognizing these typical resource constraints and employing thoughtful strategies, organizations can find practical ways to balance quality and quantity without compromising their standards.

Resistance to Change

Organizational Inertia

Organizational inertia refers to the tendency of companies or institutions to resist change, even when it's necessary for growth or improvement. This inertia can be deeply ingrained in an organization's culture, often stemming from a preference for maintaining the status quo. For businesses seeking to strike a balance between quality and quantity, this resistance can prevent them from adopting new systems, processes, or technologies that could improve both.

The impact of organizational inertia can be profound. Employees and management alike may be accustomed to existing workflows, even if they are inefficient or lead to suboptimal outcomes. Any suggestion of change, particularly one that involves altering long-standing practices, can be met with skepticism, reluctance, or outright opposition. This is especially true when changes necessitate reevaluation of roles, responsibilities, or performance metrics.

To successfully overcome organizational inertia, leadership must play a pivotal role in communicating the need for change and the benefits it will bring. This process often involves creating a compelling vision for the future and demonstrating how the proposed changes align with the organization's goals. Additionally, involving employees in the change process through transparent communication and active participation can help ease resistance.

For example, Toyota's lean manufacturing approach was initially met with resistance, but the company gradually overcame this inertia by emphasizing continuous improvement and employee involvement. By demonstrating the benefits of lean methodologies, such as improved efficiency and enhanced product quality, Toyota shifted its organizational culture towards embracing innovation and striking a balance between quality and quantity.

Fear of Failure

Fear of failure is another significant obstacle preventing organizations and individuals from adopting new practices that could enhance quality and output. The fear of making mistakes or being held accountable for unsuccessful initiatives can stifle innovation and experimentation. In environments where failure is viewed as a personal or organizational shortcoming, employees are less likely to propose new ideas or challenge existing practices.

This fear can lead to a culture of risk aversion, where maintaining the current methods—even if they are inefficient—feels safer than exploring new ways to improve quality and quantity. Over time, this stagnation can hinder growth and reduce competitiveness in rapidly evolving industries.

Fostering a culture of experimentation and learning is critical to overcoming this fear. Organizations that embrace failure as a natural part of the learning process are more likely to encourage innovation. Leaders can promote this mindset by celebrating efforts to improve, regardless of the outcome, and by framing failures as valuable learning experiences.

Google is an example of a company that embraces experimentation and learning. The company is known for its "moonshot thinking," which encourages high-risk projects as part of its broader innovation strategy. While not all experiments lead to success, the willingness to explore

Quality verses Quantity: Is There a Middle Way?

new ideas without fear of failure has led to groundbreaking products, such as Google Search and Android.

Organizations can also implement structured feedback loops to reduce fear of failure. In these loops, employees are encouraged to reflect on what worked, what didn't, and what can be improved. Regularly sharing lessons learned from successful and unsuccessful initiatives helps build a culture where continuous improvement is valued over the status quo.

By addressing organizational inertia and the fear of failure, businesses can create environments that are more conducive to adopting new practices and striking a balance between quality and quantity.

Market and Competitive Pressures
Maintaining Competitiveness

In fast-paced markets, companies often face pressure to produce large quantities of products or services to meet demand and stay ahead of their competitors. However, maintaining high quality while delivering the amount can be daunting, particularly when competitors focus on scaling their production capabilities or lowering prices.

The need to deliver quality while competing on quantity is particularly prevalent in consumer electronics, fashion, and food manufacturing industries. These sectors often experience rapid product cycles and evolving trends, forcing companies to produce more quickly while maintaining quality standards. In such environments, companies that sacrifice quality to increase output may find short-term success but often face long-term brand erosion, customer dissatisfaction, and increased returns or defects.

A successful approach to balancing these pressures is evident in companies that prioritize operational efficiency and strategic innovation. Apple is a prime example of a company that has mastered this balance. While producing millions of devices annually, Apple remains committed to quality by employing rigorous quality control measures and investing heavily in research and development. Apple's ability to innovate, improve processes, and focus on customer experience allows the company to remain competitive without compromising quality, even in a highly competitive market.

Another example is Toyota, which has maintained its competitive edge through its lean manufacturing system. By emphasizing continuous improvement (Kaizen) and waste reduction, Toyota has been able to produce vehicles at scale while ensuring consistent quality. This approach enhances competitiveness and positions the company as a leader in efficiency and product reliability.

Customer Expectations

Meeting customer expectations for both quality and quantity presents a unique challenge. Consumers today demand products and services that are available in large quantities and meet high-quality standards. These expectations vary widely depending on the market, product category, and customer segment. For instance, some customers prioritize affordability and quick delivery, while others focus on premium quality and craftsmanship.

The difficulty lies in managing these diverse expectations while maintaining operational efficiency. For example, in the fast fashion industry, customers expect new styles to be available frequently, but they also want longer clothing. Balancing these demands often leads to tensions between speed and durability. Companies that focus too heavily on one aspect risk alienating a portion of their customer base.

A strategy for managing customer expectations effectively involves transparent communication and setting realistic expectations. Companies like Patagonia, which emphasize sustainability and quality, manage customer expectations by aligning their brand values with delivery. They communicate their commitment to long-lasting, environmentally friendly products, which resonate with customers who value quality over fast consumption.

Another effective strategy is offering a range of product lines that cater to different customer needs. Many tech companies provide high-end and budget-friendly options, enabling them to meet diverse customer expectations while maintaining their competitive edge. Samsung, for instance, offers both flagship smartphones with cutting-edge features and more affordable models, ensuring they address the needs of both premium and cost-conscious customers.

Additionally, aligning marketing efforts with the company's quality and quantity goals helps manage customer expectations. When customers understand a brand's value proposition, whether it's based on speed, quality, or a combination of both, they are more likely to align their expectations with what the company delivers.

Ultimately, balancing customer expectations with market pressures requires a combination of operational excellence, strategic positioning, and clear communication. Companies that successfully manage these elements are better equipped to navigate the complex landscape of quality and quantity demands.

Strategies for Overcoming Obstacles

Change Management

Change management is critical to overcoming resistance and successfully implementing strategies that balance quality and quantity. By adopting key management principles, organizations can create smoother transitions, foster stakeholder acceptance, and implement new processes effectively.

Principles of Change Management

The following principles are essential to any successful management change:

> - **Communication:** Clear and consistent communication is the backbone of any change initiative. Explaining the what and how of the change and the why is vital. People are more likely to accept change when they understand its rationale, especially if it is tied to improving quality and quantity. Regular updates, open forums for feedback, and transparency throughout the process help to build trust and mitigate resistance.
>
> - **Stakeholder Engagement:** Engaging all relevant stakeholders, from top leadership to frontline employees, ensures that the

voices of those affected by the change are heard. Involving stakeholders early helps address concerns, create buy-in, and provide valuable insights into potential obstacles. When people feel involved in the process, they are more likely to support the changes, leading to smoother implementation.

➤ **Training and Support:** Change is often accompanied by the need for new skills, especially when balancing quality and quantity requires new tools, technologies, or processes. Providing comprehensive training helps ease the transition and ensures that staff are well-equipped to meet the demands of the new system. Ongoing support is also crucial, as challenges may arise during adjustment. Offering resources, mentoring, and troubleshooting assistance reinforces employees' confidence as they adapt.

Applying these principles can significantly reduce resistance to change and increase the likelihood of a successful balance between quality and quantity. For example, an organization transitioning to a lean manufacturing model must ensure that communication flows freely across all departments, that employees are engaged in identifying inefficiencies, and that comprehensive training is provided on lean principles.

Successful Change Initiatives

Several organizations have successfully implemented change management strategies to strike a balance between quality and quantity, offering valuable lessons and best practices.

One standout example is **General Electric (GE)** during the implementation of Six Sigma in the 1990s. At the time, GE sought to improve quality while scaling production. The key to their success was a robust management approach, which included clear communication from leadership, strong stakeholder engagement, and comprehensive training programs for employees at all levels. The initiative led to significant improvements in both process efficiency and product quality. Lessons from this case underscore the importance of leadership involvement in driving change and the necessity of comprehensive training to develop the skills necessary for success.

Another example is **Nissan**, which struggled with inefficiencies and declining market share in the early 2000s. Under the leadership of CEO Carlos Ghosn, the company underwent a radical transformation, focusing on improving quality and increasing output. The change initiative emphasized transparent communication with employees and external stakeholders, stakeholder involvement in decision-making, and substantial investment in workforce development. The result was a leaner, more agile organization capable of producing high-quality vehicles at scale. Nissan's turnaround demonstrated the importance of aligning change initiatives with strategic business goals and ensuring continuous stakeholder engagement.

These case studies demonstrate the effectiveness of applying change management principles in overcoming obstacles, striking a balance between quality and quantity, and achieving long-term success. By cultivating a culture of open communication, engagement, and continuous learning, organizations can navigate the complexities of change and emerge stronger.

Innovation and Adaptation

Embracing New Technologies

In today's fast-evolving marketplace, adopting new technologies is crucial for companies seeking to improve quality and efficiency. Technological innovation enables businesses to optimize processes, minimize errors, and enhance productivity while upholding high-quality standards. Integrating automation, artificial intelligence (AI), machine learning, and advanced analytics has proven transformative for many industries, helping them to navigate the challenge of balancing quality with quantity.

One prominent example of successful technology adoption is **Tesla**. As an electric vehicle manufacturer, Tesla has adopted cutting-edge technologies, such as AI-driven automation in its production lines, enabling it to scale up production while maintaining the precision and quality required for complex vehicles. Tesla's use of robotics and AI-enabled systems has optimized the assembly process, minimized defects, and increased output speed. This balance between technological advancement and quality control has positioned Tesla as a leader in both innovation and efficiency in the automotive industry.

Another example is **Amazon**, which leverages robotics and AI to manage logistics operations. With warehouses worldwide, Amazon faces the challenge of fulfilling many orders quickly while ensuring that each item is accurately processed and delivered in top condition. By utilizing robotics to automate sorting, packing, and inventory management, Amazon strikes a remarkable balance between speed and quality, thereby reducing errors and enhancing customer satisfaction.

Incorporating technology into the workflow streamlines production and allows continuous improvement. Companies that proactively embrace technological advancements are better positioned to maintain competitiveness in fast-paced markets while ensuring that quality standards are met or exceeded.

Agile Methodologies
Agile methodologies have become increasingly popular as organizations seek to remain flexible and responsive to market changes without compromising quality. Initially developed for the software industry, agile principles focus on iterative development, collaboration, and continuous feedback. These practices allow teams to adjust quickly to new information or changing requirements while maintaining high performance.

Agile methodologies are particularly valuable for organizations that must balance quality with quantity in rapidly changing environments. Agile teams can ensure that quality is maintained at every production stage by breaking projects into smaller increments, or sprints, and focusing on delivering a usable product at the end of each sprint. The iterative nature of agile allows for continuous improvement and course correction, helping organizations stay aligned with internal quality standards and external market demands.

For example, **Spotify** uses agile methodologies to manage its product development process. The company's structure is designed around agile squads that work on different app features. This approach enables Spotify to continuously release updates and new features while maintaining the app's stability and user-friendliness. By focusing on short development cycles and incorporating user feedback, Spotify maintains high product quality while delivering frequent updates to millions of users.

Similarly, **Microsoft** employs agile methodologies in developing its cloud services, particularly Azure. By utilizing agile methods, Microsoft's development teams can effectively respond to evolving customer needs and industry trends, releasing updates and improvements on a regular basis. This adaptability enables Microsoft to compete in the cloud while ensuring its services maintain high reliability and security.

Agile methodologies emphasize collaboration, transparency, and iterative progress, making them highly effective for organizations seeking to balance quality and quantity. Whether in product development, marketing, or manufacturing, agility enables companies to respond to market shifts while maintaining a commitment to excellence.

By embracing new technologies and adopting agile practices, organizations can foster innovation, enhance efficiency, and achieve sustainable success in striking a balance between quality and quantity.

Resource Optimization

Efficient Resource Allocation

Optimizing the use of resources is crucial for organizations seeking to strike a balance between quality and quantity. Efficient resource allocation ensures that financial and human resources are utilized effectively, resulting in higher productivity and better-quality outcomes. Several strategies, including lean principles, just-in-time (JIT) inventory management, and strategic outsourcing, have been proven to optimize resource utilization without compromising quality.

- **Lean Principles:** Lean manufacturing principles emphasize reducing waste and enhancing efficiency throughout all processes. Organizations can allocate resources more effectively by eliminating non-value-adding activities, leading to improved output and quality. Lean emphasizes continuous improvement (Kaizen), encouraging teams to assess and refine their processes regularly. One notable example of lean in action is **Toyota**, which pioneered lean manufacturing. Through its Toyota Production System (TPS), the company reduced waste, improved workflow efficiency, and maintained high-quality standards while scaling production. This approach enabled Toyota to remain competitive while consistently delivering high-quality products.

- **Just-in-Time (JIT) Inventory:** JIT is another powerful strategy for optimizing resource allocation. Organizations can reduce storage costs and waste by producing goods only as needed and minimizing excess inventory. This system requires precise coordination between suppliers and manufacturers to ensure that materials arrive just as necessary for production. **Dell**, for instance, utilized JIT inventory to streamline its manufacturing process, assembling computers only after an order was placed. This allowed the company to minimize inventory costs while delivering customized, high-quality products at scale.

- **Strategic Outsourcing:** Outsourcing non-core activities enables organizations to focus their internal resources on areas that directly impact quality and innovation. By partnering with specialized vendors for logistics, customer support, or IT services, companies can enhance operational efficiency and free up resources for product development and quality assurance. **Nike** is a well-known example of a company that has effectively utilized outsourcing for its manufacturing needs. While maintaining control over design and innovation, Nike outsources production to partners worldwide, allowing the company to scale output while ensuring high-quality products through rigorous standards and oversight.

Quality verses Quantity: Is There a Middle Way?

Organizations can optimize resource allocation by adopting these strategies, improving productivity and quality while remaining agile and competitive.

Training and Development

Continuous training and development are critical for closing skills gaps and ensuring the workforce is equipped to meet current and future challenges. An organization's ability to balance quality and quantity is closely tied to the capabilities of its employees. As technology and market demands evolve, so must the workforce's skill sets.

Investing in training programs enhances employee competencies, boosts morale, and increases job satisfaction, ultimately leading to greater productivity and a higher quality of work. Additionally, training programs can help employees adapt to new technologies and methodologies, such as automation or agile workflows, that are essential for balancing quality and quantity.

One example of an effective training program is **Amazon's Career Choice Program**, which allows employees to learn new skills and earn certifications in information technology, healthcare, and advanced manufacturing. By investing in employee development, Amazon helps its workforce stay competitive while ensuring they can meet the company's evolving needs. This investment in training aligns with Amazon's broader strategy of maintaining high productivity and quality in its operations.

Another successful example is **AT&T's Future Ready program**, which focuses on reskilling and upskilling its workforce to meet the demands of the digital age. AT&T provides employees access to courses in data science, cybersecurity, and other high-demand fields, ensuring the company has a skilled workforce capable of navigating technological shifts while maintaining service quality.

Continuous training addresses immediate skills gaps and builds a culture of learning and improvement. This culture enables organizations to remain adaptable and prepared to strike a balance between quality and quantity as market conditions change.

By optimizing resource allocation and investing in training and development, organizations can strengthen their ability to achieve high-quality outcomes and efficient production, ensuring sustainable success in a competitive marketplace.

Potential Benefits of Finding a Middle Way

Enhanced Sustainability

One of the most compelling advantages of striking a balance between quality and quantity is the potential for enhanced sustainability. When organizations strike a balance, they improve operational efficiency and contribute to a more sustainable future—both economically and environmentally.

Long-Term Viability

Balancing quality and quantity is crucial for the long-term viability of businesses and organizations. Companies that emphasize both aspects are better positioned to thrive in shifting market conditions, consumer expectations, and competitive pressures. Organizations can sustain steady growth and maintain customer loyalty by avoiding the pitfalls of focusing too heavily on one side—such as sacrificing quality for higher output or limiting growth potential by prioritizing quality alone.

Businesses focusing on long-term viability through balanced strategies often adopt sustainable practices that integrate high-quality outputs and scalable processes. For example, the outdoor clothing company Patagonia has built its brand around durable, high-quality products designed to withstand the test of time. By committing to quality, Patagonia reduces the frequency customers need to replace items, aligning with its mission to promote sustainability. At the same time, Patagonia ensures that it can scale production to meet growing demand, demonstrating how striking a balance between quality and quantity contributes to long-term business success.

Another example is **Unilever**, a global leader in consumer goods, which has adopted a sustainable business model that balances product quality with responsible growth. Through its *Sustainable Living Plan*, Unilever focuses on improving the health and well-being of consumers, reducing its environmental impact, and enhancing the livelihoods of people across its supply chain. By embedding sustainability into its core business strategy, Unilever ensures that it remains viable in the long term while continuing to produce high-quality products at scale.

Environmental Responsibility

Finding a middle way also leads to significant environmental benefits. Sustainable practices that strike a balance between quality and quantity reduce waste, optimize resource use, and improve production processes, all of which have a positive impact on the environment.

Reducing waste is a key element of environmental responsibility. When organizations prioritize quality alongside quantity, they often focus on reducing defective products, overproduction, and excess inventory. For example, companies that adopt **circular economy** models, like **IKEA**, aim to minimize waste by designing products that can be reused, recycled, or refurbished. This approach minimizes environmental impact and ensures that resources are utilized more efficiently throughout the product's lifecycle.

Additionally, businesses that optimize resource allocation through sustainable practices contribute to environmental sustainability. Companies can utilize resources such as water, energy, and raw materials more efficiently to minimize their environmental impact while maintaining high production levels. The **automotive industry** offers a strong example, with companies like **BMW** implementing energy-efficient manufacturing processes that reduce carbon emissions while ensuring vehicle quality. Through investments in renewable energy and sustainable materials, BMW has found a middle way that balances the need for high production volumes with environmental responsibility.

Companies like Stella McCartney have set new standards for environmentally responsible practices in industries such as fashion, where fast production cycles can result in significant waste. McCartney's brand emphasizes the use of sustainable materials and ethical production methods, while maintaining a high standard of product quality. By doing so, the brand reduces the environmental impact of its manufacturing processes, proving that fashion can be both stylish and sustainable.

Businesses that adopt sustainable practices through balanced strategies contribute to the organization's long-term health and play a vital role in environmental stewardship. By reducing waste, optimizing resources, and committing to responsible growth, these companies demonstrate how striking a balance between quality and quantity can enhance sustainability in meaningful ways.

Employee Satisfaction and Retention

Workforce Engagement

Balancing quality and quantity is beneficial for business operations and plays a significant role in enhancing employee satisfaction and engagement. When organizations prioritize both aspects, employees often experience a more rewarding work environment, as they can take pride in the quality of their contributions while being part of a team that achieves tangible results on a scale.

High-quality work fosters a sense of purpose and fulfillment among employees, connecting them to the organization's broader goals. When quantity is emphasized—without compromising quality—employees gain an understanding of accomplishment, knowing that their efforts lead to meaningful outcomes. This balance prevents burnout and frustration when employees are pressured to produce more without regard for quality, or conversely, when they feel limited by an overemphasis on perfectionism at the expense of achieving results.

Organizations that strongly focus on striking a balance between quality and quantity tend to have higher employee retention rates. For example, Google has long been recognized for creating an environment that values innovation (quality) and efficiency (quantity). Google's employees feel empowered and productive through creative autonomy and structured goals. This focus on balance contributes to high levels of employee satisfaction and a strong sense of engagement, resulting in consistently low turnover rates.

Another example is **Southwest Airlines**, which fosters a culture that encourages employees to deliver high-quality service while maintaining operational efficiency. Southwest emphasizes teamwork, communication, and a strong commitment to customer satisfaction, all of which contribute to the airline's success in balancing the demands of quality service and operational scale. This balanced approach has led to high employee engagement and one of the lowest turnover rates in the industry.

Professional Development

Continuous improvement and professional development are crucial to creating a positive work environment and fostering employee growth. When organizations invest in their employees through ongoing training, skill development, and opportunities for advancement, they contribute to higher job satisfaction and improved long-term employee retention.

Professional development also plays a crucial role in bridging the gap between quality and quantity. As employees enhance their skills and learn new methodologies, they become more efficient and capable of delivering high-quality work more quickly. This creates a positive feedback loop, where continuous improvement benefits the organization and contributes to the personal growth and fulfillment of its employees.

Companies prioritizing professional development often enjoy higher employee loyalty and engagement levels. For example, **IBM** invests heavily in its upskilling workforce through programs such as its *You're Learning* platform, which offers employees access to personalized learning opportunities. IBM's commitment to continuous learning ensures that employees are equipped to meet the demands of the ever-changing tech industry, helping the company maintain a highly skilled and motivated workforce.

Similarly, **Salesforce** focuses on employee development through its *Trailhead* learning platform, which provides employees with opportunities to acquire new skills, earn certifications, and advance in their careers. By offering continuous education and professional development, Salesforce fosters a culture of growth that translates into higher employee satisfaction and retention.

Investing in professional development also creates a culture of trust and loyalty, as employees feel valued and supported in their career journeys. This, in turn, leads to greater engagement, better job performance, and longer tenure within the organization.

Balancing quality and quantity benefits organizational performance, creating a work environment that enhances employee satisfaction and retention. By fostering engagement and providing opportunities for professional growth, organizations can build a motivated workforce committed to delivering high-quality results on a larger scale.

Customer Loyalty and Brand Reputation

Building Trust and Loyalty

In today's competitive marketplace, customer loyalty is built on trust. High-quality products and services, delivered consistently and efficiently, are key to establishing that trust. Customers who rely on a brand to meet or exceed their expectations are more likely to return, recommend the brand to others, and develop loyalty that transcends short-term market trends.

A balance between quality and quantity plays a crucial role in this equation. When a company can deliver products or services on a scale without compromising quality, it reinforces customer confidence. Reliable delivery times and superior products create a positive customer experience that fosters loyalty. This is particularly important in industries where customers expect both speed and excellence, such as e-commerce, consumer goods, and the hospitality sector.

One well-known example of a brand with a loyal customer base built on trust and quality is **Apple**. Apple's products, including iPhones, MacBooks, and Apple Watches, are known for their premium quality, sleek design, and user-friendly features. Despite producing millions of units annually, Apple maintains stringent quality control, which reassures customers that they are investing in products that will deliver value over time. The brand's reputation for quality and reliability has created an incredibly loyal customer base, with many purchasing new Apple products without hesitation.

Another example is **Starbucks**, which has built customer loyalty through high-quality coffee and efficient service. Despite being a global chain with thousands of locations, Starbucks maintains a commitment to delivering a consistent, premium experience, from the taste of the coffee to the ambiance of its stores. Customers trust that they will receive the same high-quality product, regardless of location, which reinforces their loyalty to the brand.

Positive Brand Image

Maintaining a balance between quality and quantity also enhances a company's brand reputation. A positive brand image is often the result of a company's long-term commitment to quality, even as it scales to meet growing demand. Companies that successfully manage this balance are usually viewed as trustworthy, reliable, and customer-focused, strengthening their brand presence.

For instance, **Patagonia** has earned a positive brand image by adhering to sustainable business practices while producing high-quality outdoor gear. Patagonia's commitment to quality and its focus on environmental responsibility has attracted a loyal customer base and bolstered its reputation as a purpose-driven company. This balance between quality, sustainability, and scalability has allowed Patagonia to stand out in the crowded outdoor apparel market, earning it widespread praise for its ethical approach.

Similarly, **Tesla** has cultivated a strong brand image by striking a balance between innovation, product quality, and scalability. Despite the rapid growth in production to meet increasing global demand for electric vehicles, Tesla has maintained its reputation for cutting-edge technology and high-performance vehicles. Tesla's focus on quality and commitment to sustainable energy has solidified its brand as an automotive and clean energy leader.

These examples demonstrate how a commitment to quality and quantity contributes to a brand's long-term reputation. By consistently delivering high-quality products at scale, companies build a positive brand image that resonates with customers, reinforces trust, and differentiates them from competitors.

Balancing quality and quantity is crucial in building customer loyalty and enhancing brand reputation. By consistently delivering products and services that meet high standards, companies can earn customer trust, foster loyalty, and establish a strong, positive brand image in the marketplace.

Future Trends and Opportunities

Technological Advancements

As industries evolve, technological advancements such as artificial intelligence (AI), automation, and data-driven decision-making are playing an increasingly critical role in helping businesses strike a balance between quality and quantity. These technologies provide powerful tools for optimizing operations, enhancing efficiency, and maintaining high standards of quality, all while scaling to meet demand.

AI and Automation

Artificial intelligence (AI) and automation are revolutionizing industries by streamlining processes, reducing human error, and enhancing both quality and quantity in production. Automation enables businesses to increase output without sacrificing precision, while AI facilitates informed decision-making and predictive maintenance, ensuring that quality is maintained throughout the production process.

In manufacturing, **BMW** uses AI and automation to optimize production lines while maintaining strict quality controls. BMW's assembly plants employ robots to handle repetitive tasks, such as welding and painting, with unmatched precision, reducing the likelihood of defects. AI is also integrated into the inspection process, using advanced image recognition to detect flaws that may not be visible to the human eye. This combination of AI and automation enables BMW to produce high volumes of vehicles without compromising on the quality of craftsmanship, contributing to the company's reputation for engineering excellence.

In retail and e-commerce, **Amazon** relies heavily on automation and AI to streamline its logistics and delivery networks. Automated systems manage inventory and fulfillment in Amazon's warehouses, allowing for faster order processing and reducing the risk of human error. AI algorithms help optimize delivery routes, ensuring customers receive orders quickly and accurately. By leveraging AI and automation, Amazon maintains a high standard of service while managing an enormous volume of transactions daily.

These examples demonstrate how AI and automation are crucial to future business success, enabling organizations to scale their operations while maintaining product and service quality.

Data-Driven Decision Making

Data analytics and predictive modeling have become essential tools for optimizing operations and enhancing quality and efficiency. With the advent of big data, businesses now have access to vast amounts of information that can be analyzed to make informed, real-time decisions. This data-driven approach enables organizations to identify patterns, forecast trends, and refine processes to enhance productivity and quality.

For example, **Procter & Gamble (P&G)** uses data analytics to optimize its supply chain, ensuring it can meet demand while minimizing waste and maintaining high product standards. P&G's data-driven approach involves analyzing historical sales data, market trends, and consumer behavior to predict demand and adjust production schedules accordingly. By relying on predictive modeling, the company can ensure that it produces the correct quantity of products at the right time without overproducing or compromising quality.

Similarly, **UPS** employs data analytics to enhance its logistics operations. By analyzing real-time data from its delivery network, UPS can optimize routes, reduce fuel consumption, and ensure packages are delivered on time. This use of data-driven decision-making enables UPS to strike a balance between the need for speed and efficiency and the company's commitment to providing reliable, high-quality service.

Harnessing data for strategic decision-making is becoming increasingly important across industries. Companies that embrace data analytics are better equipped to respond to market fluctuations, optimize resource allocation, and deliver high-quality products and services efficiently.

In summary, technological advancements such as AI, automation, and data-driven decision-making provide businesses with powerful tools to strike a balance between quality and quantity. By embracing these technologies, companies can enhance their operations, scale efficiently, and maintain high standards, thereby positioning themselves for future success in an increasingly competitive landscape.

Sustainability and Ethical Practices

Circular Economy Models

The circular economy is an innovative model that seeks to minimize waste and maximize resource use by rethinking how products are designed, used, and disposed of. Unlike the traditional linear economy, which follows a "take, make, dispose" model, the circular economy emphasizes reuse, recycling, and regeneration. This approach enables businesses to strike a balance between quality and quantity by extending the lifecycle of products while optimizing resource utilization.

In a circular economy, companies focus on designing products that can be easily repaired, reused, or recycled, thereby minimizing waste and promoting sustainability. This reduces waste and ensures that the quality of products remains high throughout their extended lifespan. By adopting circular practices, businesses can scale production without increasing their environmental footprint.

One leading example is **IKEA**, which has adopted the principles of the circular economy by designing furniture that can be easily disassembled, repaired, or recycled. IKEA aims to become a fully circular business by 2030, ensuring all products are made from renewable or recycled materials. By promoting product durability and encouraging customers to repair or repurpose furniture rather than discard it, IKEA demonstrates how circular economy models can help balance quality and quantity while minimizing environmental impact.

Another company adopting circular economy practices is **the Ellen MacArthur Foundation, which collaborates with businesses across** various industries to promote circular solutions. **By partnering with companies like H&M and Unilever, the foundation has helped** integrate circular practices into supply chains, from sustainable material sourcing to waste reduction and product recycling. These efforts demonstrate how circular models can improve product quality and operational efficiency while minimizing environmental impact.

Corporate Social Responsibility (CSR)

Corporate social responsibility (CSR) has become an essential element of business strategy for companies seeking to balance quality and quantity while contributing to societal well-being. CSR initiatives address the social, environmental, and ethical impacts of business operations, ensuring that companies operate in a manner that benefits their stakeholders and the broader community.

Integrating CSR into business strategies helps companies maintain high product standards while addressing labor practices, environmental sustainability, and community engagement. When companies prioritize ethical practices and responsible growth, they often gain customer trust and loyalty, reinforcing their ability to scale without compromising quality.

One example of successful CSR integration is **Ben & Jerry's**, the ice cream company known for its strong commitment to social and environmental causes. Ben & Jerry's sources fair-trade ingredients, ensures its suppliers uphold ethical labor practices and invest in renewable energy. By embedding CSR into its business model, the company demonstrates that it can produce high-quality products at scale while positively impacting society.

Levi Strauss & Co. is another company that has successfully integrated CSR into its operations. Levi's has made sustainability a core part of its strategy by reducing water usage in manufacturing, promoting ethical labor practices, and encouraging customers to recycle their old jeans through its in-store recycling program. These CSR efforts help Levi's maintain high product standards and build a positive brand image as a company that cares about both people and the planet.

Companies can strike a balance between quality and quantity by embracing CSR and circular economy models, thereby promoting ethical and sustainable practices. These approaches ensure long-term business success by aligning growth with responsible corporate behavior, making them vital for the future of business.

Reflection on Challenges and Opportunities

Summary of Key Points

This chapter explores the common obstacles to balancing quality and quantity, as well as the strategies organizations and individuals can use to overcome them. We discussed how resource constraints, whether financial, temporal, or workforce-related, can impede efforts to achieve this balance but also highlighted ways to address these limitations through optimized resource allocation, effective time management, and training. Resistance to change, market pressures, and competitive forces, as well as the need for innovation, were also examined, focusing on how change management principles, technological advancements, and agile methodologies can help overcome these challenges.

We also examined the potential benefits of finding a middle ground, including enhanced sustainability, improved employee satisfaction, stronger customer loyalty, and a positive brand image. By adopting circular economy models and integrating corporate social responsibility (CSR) into their strategies, businesses can strike a balance between quality and quantity, contributing to environmental sustainability and ethical practices.

Encouragement for Embracing Opportunities

Balancing quality and quantity presents vast and impactful opportunities. By addressing the obstacles outlined in this chapter, individuals and organizations can unlock long-term sustainability, enhance operational efficiency, and foster environments where innovation thrives. Embracing this balance leads to more engaged employees, satisfied customers, and a stronger brand reputation—benefits that ripple across society.

Quality verses Quantity: Is There a Middle Way?

Finding a balance between quality and quantity can transform an organization, ensuring it remains competitive in an ever-evolving market. For individuals, this balance leads to greater satisfaction in their personal and professional lives as they learn to prioritize both excellence and productivity. On a broader scale, adopting sustainable practices benefits businesses and contributes to a more responsible and equitable world.

As you move forward, I encourage you to embrace the opportunities of finding this balance. Whether leading a business, managing a team, or navigating your personal life, pursuing quality and quantity is not an either-or choice. Instead, it is a pathway to greater fulfillment, resilience, and success.

Quality verses Quantity: Is There a Middle Way?

Case Studies and Personal Stories

Success Stories – Organizations Achieving Balance

Google: Balancing Innovation with Efficiency

Google is widely recognized for its ability to foster a culture of innovation while maintaining operational efficiency globally. One key policy that exemplifies this balance is Google's *20%-time* initiative. This policy allows employees to dedicate 20% of their work time to passion projects that may not be directly related to their core job responsibilities. By enabling employees to explore creative ideas, Google fosters an environment where innovation thrives, leading to high-quality outcomes.

The success of this policy is evident in several groundbreaking products, including Gmail, Google News, and AdSense, all of which originated from 20% time projects. This approach encourages creativity and ensures that Google maintains a continuous pipeline of innovative solutions while staying efficient in its core operations. By allowing employees the flexibility to explore their interests, Google effectively balances the drive for innovation with the need for high-quality, scalable results.

Additionally, Google's use of advanced data analytics and automation helps streamline operations, enabling the company to handle massive amounts of information while ensuring accuracy and reliability. This balance between innovation and efficiency has helped Google maintain its leadership position in the tech industry, while its commitment to quality has reinforced customer trust and loyalty.

Toyota: Lean Principles and Large-Scale Production

Toyota's success in balancing quality and quantity can be attributed to its pioneering use of Lean manufacturing principles through the *Toyota*

Production System (TPS)*. TPS emphasizes waste reduction, continuous improvement (Kaizen), and respect for people, all of which contribute to maintaining high-quality standards while scaling production efficiently. Toyota's focus on eliminating non-value-adding activities and optimizing processes enables the company to produce vehicles on a large scale without compromising attention to detail.

One of the key components of TPS is the concept of *just-in-time* (JIT) production, where materials and components are delivered precisely when they are needed in the production process. This minimizes waste and reduces inventory costs, allowing Toyota to maintain efficiency while ensuring that each vehicle meets stringent quality standards. Additionally, TPS promotes *jidoka*, or automation with a human touch, which involves empowering workers to halt production if a quality issue arises, ensuring that defects are addressed immediately.

The impact of TPS on the automotive industry is profound. Toyota's approach has been adopted by companies worldwide in manufacturing and across sectors where efficiency and quality are critical. Toyota's ability to achieve this balance has helped solidify its reputation as a leader in quality and operational excellence, making it one of the most respected automotive brands globally.

Patagonia: Commitment to Environmental Sustainability and High-Quality Products

Patagonia is a prime example of how a company can balance the production of high-quality products with a strong commitment to environmental sustainability. Known for its durable outdoor gear, Patagonia has built a brand that prioritizes ecological responsibility, ethical sourcing, and long-lasting products. This focus has strengthened the company's brand reputation and fostered a loyal customer base that aligns with Patagonia's values.

Patagonia's commitment to quality is evident in its *Worn Wear* program, which encourages customers to repair and reuse their gear rather than replace it. The company provides repair guides, sells used Patagonia items, and offers repair services, all of which contribute to reducing waste and promoting sustainable consumption. At the same time,

Quality verses Quantity: Is There a Middle Way?

Patagonia continues to produce high-quality products made from sustainable materials, ensuring that each item meets the company's rigorous standards for performance and durability.

Patagonia's focus on sustainability also extends to its supply chain, with initiatives that utilize recycled materials and reduce water and energy consumption during manufacturing. Patagonia has cultivated a brand that resonates with environmentally conscious consumers by maintaining a strong ethical stance while delivering premium products. This balance between sustainability and quality has enhanced its reputation and positioned Patagonia as a leader in the outdoor apparel industry.

Companies like Google, Toyota, and Patagonia demonstrate that it is possible to strike a balance between quality and quantity. Through innovative policies, lean principles, and a commitment to sustainability, these organizations have achieved success by fostering environments where excellence and efficiency coexist.

Individuals Striking a Balance

Entrepreneurs: Balancing Quality and Quantity in Business Ventures

Entrepreneurs often face the challenge of scaling their ventures while maintaining the quality of their products or services. The ability to strike this balance can be critical in determining a business's long-term success. Several entrepreneurs have successfully navigated these challenges, leveraging innovative strategies to achieve high-quality outcomes and scalable growth.

One prominent example is Elon Musk, the founder of Tesla and SpaceX. Musk's ventures are known for their groundbreaking innovation and commitment to high-quality standards. At Tesla, focusing on producing electric vehicles that combine top-tier performance with sustainability has helped the company scale production while maintaining a reputation for excellence. Musk's approach to balancing quality and quantity is rooted in continuous improvement, with a strong emphasis on research, development, and precision in engineering. Despite the challenges of scaling a manufacturing company, Tesla has produced high volumes of vehicles without compromising on innovation or quality, solidifying its position as a leader in the electric vehicle market.

Another example is Sara Blakely, the founder of Spanx. Blakely's entrepreneurial journey is a testament to the importance of quality in creating a successful business. From the outset, Blakely focused on designing shapewear that provided women with superior comfort and performance. As Spanx grew from a small startup to a global brand, Blakely remained committed to the original vision of high-quality products, ensuring that each new product maintained the brand's core values. This focus on quality and strategic expansion into new markets allowed Spanx to scale rapidly while building customer trust and loyalty.

Entrepreneurs who successfully balance quality and quantity often employ strategies such as investing in technology, streamlining production processes, and maintaining strong oversight over product development. These approaches enable them to meet growing demand without sacrificing the quality that sets their products apart.

Artists and Craftsmen: Dedication to Craft and Commercial Success

For many artists and artisans, the pursuit of quality is a central aspect of their work. However, achieving commercial success while maintaining the integrity of their craft can be challenging. Several individuals have struck this balance, gaining recognition for their artistry and success in the marketplace.

One notable example is Tom Ford, a fashion designer who combined artistic excellence with commercial success. Known for his meticulous attention to detail and commitment to high-quality materials, Ford's collections are celebrated for their elegance and craftsmanship. At the same time, Ford has expanded its brand into various product lines, including ready-to-wear clothing, accessories, and cosmetics, without compromising on quality. His dedication to his craft has earned him a loyal following and made his brand a global success in the highly competitive fashion industry.

Another example is Yo-Yo Ma, the world-renowned cellist, who has built a career that balances artistic integrity with widespread appeal. While Ma is known for his deep commitment to the quality of his performances, he has also embraced innovation by exploring new genres and collaborating with diverse artists. This willingness to innovate has enabled Ma to reach a broader audience while maintaining the highest standards of musicianship. His career demonstrates that prioritizing quality can coexist with achieving commercial success and reaching a broad audience.

In the world of fine craftsmanship, George Nakashima, an influential woodworker and furniture maker, stands out as someone who blended artistic dedication with business success. Nakashima was known for his mastery of wood, creating handcrafted furniture pieces that were both functional and aesthetically beautiful. His attention to quality and a deep respect for the materials he worked with earned him international acclaim and a thriving business. Despite the labor-intensive nature of his work, Nakashima managed to scale his production by training apprentices who upheld his standards, allowing his legacy to continue while maintaining the craftsmanship for which he was known.

These artists and artisans show that commercial success can be achieved without compromising quality. Through dedication to their craft, innovation, and strategic business approaches, they have built successful careers while staying true to their values.

Whether in entrepreneurship or the arts, individuals who successfully balance quality and quantity often rely on a combination of passion, innovation, and innovative strategies. Their stories provide valuable lessons on achieving success without compromising the integrity of their work.

Learning from Failures

Organizations Facing Challenges

Volkswagen Emissions Scandal: Compromising Quality Under Pressure

The Volkswagen emissions scandal, also known as "Dieselgate," is a stark example of what can happen when an organization prioritizes production speed, market share, and profit over quality and ethical standards. In 2015, it was revealed that Volkswagen had installed software in millions of diesel vehicles that allowed them to pass emissions tests while emitting far higher levels of pollutants in real-world driving conditions. The scandal significantly affected Volkswagen's reputation, legal standing, and financial health.

At the heart of the scandal was Volkswagen's desire to dominate the diesel market in the United States and Europe, where stricter emissions regulations were being enforced. The company faced intense pressure to produce a large number of vehicles that met both consumer demands for performance and environmental standards. However, instead of investing in research and development to create cleaner, compliant engines, Volkswagen used software that falsified emissions test results.

The compromise of quality in favor of quantity and market dominance led to widespread repercussions. Volkswagen faced billions of dollars in fines, legal settlements, recall costs, and irreparable damage to its brand and consumer trust. The scandal serves as a cautionary tale about the dangers of compromising quality, particularly when ethical and safety standards are at risk.

Lessons learned from the Volkswagen emissions scandal include the importance of transparency, accountability, and ethical decision-making in business operations. Companies that fail to maintain these principles may achieve short-term gains but often face long-term consequences that outweigh any temporary successes. Volkswagen's case highlights the need for organizations to balance production goals with a commitment to quality and integrity, ensuring that shortcuts in one area don't lead to catastrophic failures elsewhere.

Boeing 737 Max: The Impact of Speed Over Quality Control
Another example of failure to balance quality and quantity is the Boeing 737 Max crisis. The 737 Max was a new version of Boeing's highly successful 737 line, developed to compete with Airbus in the commercial aviation market. However, the aircraft was grounded worldwide in 2019 after two fatal crashes that killed 346 people. The

Quality verses Quantity: Is There a Middle Way?

crashes were linked to a software malfunction in the Maneuvering Characteristics Augmentation System (MCAS). This feature was designed to prevent the aircraft from stalling but contributed to losing control in both crashes.

The Boeing 737 Max case highlights the tension between production speed and quality control. Boeing was pressured to deliver the 737 Max quickly to compete with Airbus's A320neo, which had captured significant market share due to its fuel efficiency. Boeing accelerated production timelines to meet deadlines and reduce costs, downplayed safety concerns, and bypassed rigorous testing and regulatory oversight for key systems like MCAS.

The consequences of prioritizing speed over safety were severe. In addition to the tragic loss of life, Boeing's reputation was severely damaged, resulting in billions of dollars in losses from legal settlements, compensation to airlines, and the costs associated with grounding the entire 737 Max fleet. Boeing's safety practices were questioned, and the company faced an uphill battle regaining the trust of regulators, airlines, and the public.

The lessons from the Boeing 737 Max crisis center around the critical importance of safety, transparency, and quality control in industries where even small compromises can have catastrophic consequences. The push to speed up production without addressing potential safety risks led to tragic outcomes and threatened Boeing's long-term viability as a leader in the aviation industry. The case highlights that striking a balance between production goals and rigorous quality standards is both desirable and essential in sectors where lives are at risk.

The Volkswagen and Boeing cases demonstrate how organizations that fail to strike a proper balance between quality and quantity face significant risks, including legal, financial, and reputational damage. These failures underscore the importance of ethical leadership, robust safety protocols, and a commitment to quality in ensuring long-term success and sustainability.

Individuals Overcoming Obstacles

Personal Stories of Burnout and Recovery

Many individuals who initially focused heavily on quantity—whether in their careers, personal lives, or creative pursuits—have experienced burnout, only to recover by rebalancing their focus on quality. These stories highlight the importance of pacing oneself and prioritizing well-being over the relentless pursuit of productivity.

One powerful example is Arianna Huffington, co-founder of The Huffington Post. In 2007, Huffington collapsed from exhaustion and broke her cheekbone, a wake-up call that led her to rethink her work habits. At the time, she was overworking herself, driven by the pressure to maintain high output and productivity. Her recovery began when she shifted her focus from quantity to quality, particularly in terms of her well-being. Huffington advocated for the importance of sleep, rest, and mindfulness, which she details in her book *Thrive*. Her experience shows that by prioritizing health and quality over constant output, individuals can achieve a more sustainable and fulfilling life without sacrificing success.

Another example is Chris Burkard, a renowned adventure photographer who faced burnout early in his career. Burkard was driven to constantly produce work and gain recognition, often at the expense of his health and relationships. After realizing the toll this was taking on his life, he restructured his approach to his work. He began to prioritize quality time with his family and focused on passion projects that resonated deeply with him rather than churning out a high volume of work. This shift helped him recover from burnout and led to some of his most meaningful and high-quality work in his career.

The lessons from these individuals' stories include setting boundaries, prioritizing self-care, and finding meaning in one's work. By focusing on the quality of their output rather than sheer quantity, they overcame burnout and achieved greater satisfaction in their personal and professional lives.

Quality verses Quantity: Is There a Middle Way?
Navigating Consumer Pressures

In today's consumer-driven world, individuals often feel the pressure to accumulate more—whether it's material possessions, achievements, or status. However, some have successfully navigated these pressures by rebalancing their focus on quality over quantity, finding greater satisfaction in minimalism, intentional living, or mindful consumption.

One well-known example is Joshua Fields Millburn and **Ryan Nicodemus**, known as *The Minimalists*. After achieving what many would consider success in their corporate careers, they realized that their focus on accumulating more money, possessions, and status was leaving them unfulfilled. Millburn and Nicodemus experienced a moment of reckoning, where they radically simplified their lives by eliminating excess possessions and focusing on what truly mattered to them. Their minimalist lifestyle enabled them to escape the pressures of consumer culture and discover a sense of purpose in living with less, focusing on higher-quality experiences, relationships, and personal growth. Through their books, documentaries, and speaking engagements, they've inspired millions to pursue quality over quantity in their own lives.

Another example is Cait Flanders, the author of *The Year of Less*. After finding herself in a cycle of debt, consumerism, and burnout, Flanders embarked on a year-long journey of not buying anything she didn't need. This experiment helped her realize how much consumer pressures had influenced her habits and how little happiness they brought her. Through this process, she found balance by focusing on quality experiences and personal growth rather than material accumulation. Her journey resonated with many who sought a more intentional and mindful approach to consumption.

These individuals employed minimalist, mindful, and intentional living strategies to overcome consumer pressures. By shifting their focus from pursuing more to pursuing better, they discovered deeper satisfaction and fulfillment in their lives. Their stories underscore the power of making conscious choices about what to prioritize, whether it be possessions, time, or personal goals.

Individuals who have overcome obstacles like burnout or consumer pressures demonstrate the value of rebalancing priorities to focus on quality. Their stories inspire others to seek greater meaning, balance, and satisfaction in their work and personal lives.

Diverse Perspectives

International Examples

Different cultures approach the balance between quality and quantity in distinct ways, shaped by their values, traditions, and economic priorities. These cultural differences offer valuable insights into how various countries manage this balance and how businesses can adapt their strategies to succeed in different contexts.

Japan's focus on quality and craftsmanship is deeply embedded in its cultural and business practices. Concepts like *kaizen* (continuous improvement) and *monozukuri* (the art of making things) reflect Japan's dedication to precision, attention to detail, and long-term excellence. This cultural emphasis is evident in automotive manufacturing, electronics, and traditional crafts industries. For instance, Japanese car manufacturers like Toyota and Honda have long prioritized quality over sheer production speed. These companies have achieved large-scale production by implementing Lean principles and the Toyota Production System (TPS) while maintaining rigorous quality standards. The Japanese approach to quality emphasizes patience, meticulousness, and a commitment to continuous improvement, creating a culture where the product is always the priority.

In contrast, **the United States** has traditionally emphasized efficiency, productivity, and scaling operations. American companies have pioneered mass production techniques, such as the assembly line, allowing for unprecedented output levels in the automotive and consumer goods industries. The focus on quantity and efficiency is rooted in the desire for growth, competitiveness, and innovation. While quality is valued, American businesses often prioritize achieving high-quality outcomes at scale through automation, technological advancements, and operational efficiency. Companies like Amazon and

Tesla exemplify the American approach, where a drive for innovation and market dominance balances an underlying commitment to quality and customer satisfaction.

These cultural differences highlight how countries approach the balance between quality and quantity. In Japan, the focus is often on refining processes and achieving mastery over time, while in the U.S., the emphasis is on scaling quickly and efficiently while maintaining a competitive edge.

Global Companies

Global companies operating in multiple markets must strive to balance quality and quantity while adapting to diverse cultural and economic contexts. Success in this area requires a profound understanding of local markets and the flexibility to tailor strategies to meet varying expectations.

One example is Unilever, a multinational consumer goods company that has successfully balanced quality and quantity across diverse markets. Unilever's global reach spans developed and emerging economies, where consumer expectations for quality and price vary significantly. In emerging markets, Unilever has adapted by offering smaller, more affordable product sizes while maintaining consistent quality in line with its global standards. This approach allows the company to cater to different economic realities without compromising its brand's reputation for high-quality products. Unilever's commitment to sustainability also enhances its global standing, as it aligns with the growing consumer preference for ethical and environmentally responsible practices.

Another example is Nestlé, one of the world's largest food and beverage companies. Nestlé's global strategy involves adapting its products to suit local tastes while maintaining rigorous quality standards. In markets like Japan, Nestlé has introduced region-specific variations of its products, such as green tea-flavored KitKats, which cater to local preferences. At the same time, Nestlé has invested heavily in ensuring that its production processes meet international quality and safety standards, regardless of location. This balance between localization and consistency has helped Nestlé maintain its position as a trusted brand in diverse markets.

Coca-Cola is another global giant that strikes a balance between quality and quantity, while adapting to diverse cultural and economic contexts. Coca-Cola's success lies in maintaining the consistency of its products worldwide while offering localized flavors and adjusting marketing strategies to resonate with different cultures. In India, for instance, Coca-Cola has introduced products like Thums Up and Maaza, which cater to local tastes while still leveraging its global distribution networks and quality control processes. This adaptability enables Coca-Cola to maintain a high level of brand recognition and trust, regardless of the market in which it operates.

Both cultural perspectives and global companies demonstrate that various factors influence the balance between quality and quantity, including cultural values, market demands, and business strategies. Companies that successfully navigate these challenges by adapting to local contexts while maintaining high-quality standards are better positioned to succeed in today's interconnected global economy.

Industry-Specific Stories

Retail (Grocery Stores): Balancing Variety and Quality

Grocery stores face the unique challenge of offering a wide variety of products while maintaining high standards of quality, particularly when handling perishable goods. This balance requires efficient supply chain management, personalized customer service, and technology for inventory control. Successful grocery stores navigate these complexities by ensuring product freshness, adapting to supply chain disruptions, and meeting consumer demand for variety and quality.

One excellent example is Whole Foods Market, which focuses on organic, sustainably sourced, high-quality products. Despite offering an extensive range of groceries, Whole Foods maintains strict quality standards, with its *Quality Standards Program* ensuring that only products that meet specific environmental and ethical sourcing criteria are stocked. Whole Foods balances quantity with quality by maintaining close relationships with suppliers and prioritizing locally sourced products, which helps to reduce supply chain issues and ensure freshness. Additionally, the company's investment in technology, such as advanced inventory management systems, allows it to monitor stock levels and predict demand more accurately, ensuring that popular items are always available without overstocking and wasting perishable goods.

Another example is Trader Joe's, which offers a curated selection of high-quality products at affordable prices. Trader Joe's limits its product range compared to larger supermarket chains, but it carefully selects products that meet strict quality standards. By reducing the number of SKUs (stock-keeping units), Trader Joe's can negotiate more favorable deals with suppliers and ensure that products meet both quality and cost expectations. The company also excels at personalized customer service, with well-trained staff offering product recommendations and insights. This focus on quality over sheer quantity helps Trader Joe's create a unique shopping experience, prioritizing freshness, quality, and customer satisfaction.

Both stores have faced challenges due to supply chain disruptions, particularly during the COVID-19 pandemic. Still, their emphasis on strong supplier relationships and efficient supply chain management allowed them to continue meeting consumer demand while maintaining quality standards. Integrating technology for inventory tracking, demand forecasting, and supplier coordination has been essential in managing disruptions and ensuring that products remain fresh and available.

Education: Balancing Depth of Knowledge and Breadth of Curriculum

Educational institutions also face the challenge of balancing the depth of knowledge with the breadth of the curriculum. Schools and universities must ensure that students gain expertise in specific subjects while acquiring broad skills that prepare them for a diverse range of career paths. Innovative approaches to curriculum design, personalized learning, and the effective use of technology have enabled many institutions to achieve this balance and enhance student outcomes.

One prominent example is Finland's education system, which has garnered global attention for its innovative approach to balancing curriculum depth with breadth. Finnish schools strongly emphasize student-centered learning, where teachers focus on the individual needs of each student rather than enforcing a rigid, standardized curriculum. While students are encouraged to explore a broad range of subjects, including the arts, sciences, and physical education, they are also allowed to dive deeper into areas that interest them. The Finnish model minimizes testing, allowing for more in-depth project-based learning, where students engage in meaningful, hands-on activities that deepen their understanding of subjects. This approach has yielded high student satisfaction and strong academic outcomes, demonstrating that striking a balance between curriculum breadth and depth can lead to well-rounded, successful students.

Another example is Harvard University, which employs an interdisciplinary approach to strike a balance between specialization and a broad educational foundation. At Harvard, students are encouraged to explore a variety of subjects during their early years before declaring a major, allowing them to gain a broad educational experience while also pursuing in-depth knowledge in their chosen fields. Harvard's *General Education Program* ensures that students are exposed to different disciplines, encouraging critical thinking and problem-solving skills applicable across fields. By combining a rigorous curriculum with the flexibility for students to explore their interests, Harvard creates an environment where quality learning is prioritized across multiple areas of study.

Integrating personalized learning and flexibility enables educational institutions to balance a broad curriculum with in-depth subject mastery. These approaches foster student engagement, creativity, and lifelong learning, while preparing students for the complexities of today's job market.

Grocery stores and educational institutions demonstrate that balancing variety and quality is achievable through strategic approaches. Whether through efficient supply chain management and personalized service in retail or innovative curriculum design in education, these sectors highlight the importance of thoughtful strategies in maintaining depth and breadth.

Practical Insights and Lessons Learned

Vision and Leadership

Strong vision and leadership are essential for striking a balance between quality and quantity in both organizational and personal pursuits. Leaders who possess a clear vision and effectively communicate it to their teams create alignment and focus, ensuring that quality standards are maintained as operations scale. This vision also provides a sense of purpose, motivating employees to strive for excellence even when facing pressures to increase output.

One common strategy successful organizations use is creating a culture where quality is non-negotiable, and leaders actively demonstrate their commitment to this standard. For instance, Apple's late co-founder, Steve Jobs, was known for his unwavering focus on product quality and user experience. He often pushed his teams to innovate and perfect products before release. His leadership ensured that Apple consistently delivered high-quality products, even as the company expanded to meet growing global demand.

Successful leaders understand the importance of empowering their teams and having a clear vision. Leaders can foster a sense of ownership and responsibility for quality and output by involving employees in decision-making processes and encouraging open feedback. This approach helps maintain high standards and promotes adaptability, as teams feel more confident in addressing challenges and proposing solutions.

Strong leadership also entails making difficult choices about priorities. Leaders who focus on long-term success over short-term gains often prioritize quality, knowing that it builds trust with customers and stakeholders. Companies like Patagonia and Toyota are examples of organizations where leadership has consistently emphasized sustainability and continuous improvement over rapid growth or mass production, enabling them to achieve a balance that sustains both quality and quantity over time.

Continuous Improvement

The principle of continuous improvement is another common theme among successful organizations and individuals who achieve balance. Successful entities understand that the journey to balance is ongoing, whether through formal processes like Lean or Six Sigma or more informal practices, such as regular feedback loops and reassessments. Continuous improvement enables organizations to refine their approaches, identify inefficiencies, and adapt to changing market conditions, ensuring that both quality and quantity can be maintained.

For instance, Toyota's Kaizen philosophy emphasizes continuous improvement at every level of the organization. This approach encourages employees to regularly assess their work processes and identify areas for improvement, whether in terms of efficiency, product quality, or resource allocation. By making incremental changes over time, Toyota consistently produces high-quality vehicles while scaling production to meet global demand. This commitment to continuous improvement has led to operational efficiency and fostered a culture of innovation that drives quality and quantity.

Similarly, companies like Amazon utilize data-driven decision-making to refine their operations continually. Regular assessments and adaptations underpin Amazon's commitment to optimizing its supply chain, improving delivery times, and enhancing customer experience. This focus on continuous improvement allows Amazon to scale efficiently while maintaining the quality of its services and products, even in the face of rapid growth and high demand.

Continuous improvement is also a hallmark of success at the individual level. Individuals who seek to balance quality and quantity often adopt habits such as self-reflection, goal setting, and feedback collection to regularly assess their progress. Entrepreneurs like Elon Musk exemplify this mindset, constantly reassessing business strategies, product designs, and market trends to improve performance and quality.

In summary, strong vision and leadership, combined with a commitment to continuous improvement, are key strategies for achieving a sustainable balance between quality and quantity. Leaders who communicate their vision, empower their teams, and prioritize long-term success set the foundation for success. Meanwhile, organizations and individuals embracing continuous improvement remain adaptable, efficient, and focused on maintaining high standards as they grow.

Actionable Takeaways

Practical Tips for Organizations

A clear strategy is essential for organizations looking to strike the right balance between quality and quantity. The following actionable tips can help businesses optimize their processes, foster leadership, and engage employees in achieving this balance:

1. **Set Clear Vision and Prioritize Quality:** Establish a clear organizational vision emphasizing quality as a non-negotiable standard. Ensure this vision is communicated consistently across all company levels, from leadership to the front lines.

2. **Empower Leaders to Make Quality-Focused Decisions:** Equip leaders with the authority and responsibility to prioritize long-term quality over short-term gains. Encourage leaders to involve teams in decision-making and emphasize the value of quality in every aspect of the business.

3. **Implement Continuous Improvement Processes:** Adopt continuous improvement frameworks, such as Lean or Six Sigma, to ensure that processes are regularly assessed and refined. Encourage employees to identify inefficiencies and propose incremental improvements that enhance efficiency and quality.

4. **Optimize Resource Allocation:** Utilize data-driven decision-making to allocate resources efficiently. Ensure that financial, material, and human resources are allocated where they can have the greatest impact on quality and quantity, with a focus on optimizing key processes.

5. **Foster Employee Engagement and Ownership:** Create a work culture where employees feel empowered to contribute to quality and output goals. Provide regular training, clear communication of goals, and opportunities for employees to offer feedback on improving processes.

6. **Leverage Technology for Efficiency and Quality Control:** Invest in technology that can streamline production processes, improve inventory management, and enhance quality control. Automation, AI, and data analytics can help organizations maintain high standards while scaling operations.

7. **Focus on Long-Term Sustainability:** Encourage leadership to prioritize sustainable growth over rapid expansion. Long-term success depends on consistently delivering high-quality products or services, which helps build customer trust and loyalty.

Practical Tips for Individuals

Individuals striving to balance quality and quantity in their personal and professional lives can use these practical strategies to enhance productivity while maintaining high standards:

1. **Set Clear Goals:** Define long-term and short-term goals emphasizing quality outcomes. Break larger tasks into manageable steps, focusing on completing each task thoroughly before moving to the next.

2. **Use Time Management Techniques:** Employ time-blocking or other time management methods to allocate specific periods for focused work. Prioritize tasks based on importance and urgency, ensuring you spend enough time on high-quality work without rushing.

3. **Embrace Continuous Learning and Improvement:** Regularly assess your progress and seek feedback from peers or mentors. Use this feedback to improve your approach to both personal and professional tasks. Continuous learning helps refine your skills and maintain a high-quality standard over time.

4. **Prioritize Self-Care:** Avoid burnout by integrating self-care into your routine. Schedule regular breaks, ensure you get enough sleep, and engage in activities that recharge your energy and creativity. Prioritizing well-being enables you to maintain high quality in both your work and life.

5. **Create Boundaries for Quality Work:** Establish clear boundaries between your professional and personal time. Allocate focused periods where you can dive deep into tasks that require high levels of attention and avoid multitasking when working on quality-driven projects.

6. **Learn to Say No:** Balancing quality and quantity sometimes means turning down opportunities or requests that stretch you too thin. Focus on the tasks and commitments that align with your goals and enable you to maintain a high standard of quality.

7. **Celebrate Small Wins:** Acknowledge your achievements, even if they are incremental. Focusing on small victories, whether completing a project with high standards or achieving a personal milestone, reinforces your commitment to quality and motivates continued growth.

Organizations and individuals can achieve a balance between quality and quantity by adopting strategies that emphasize long-term thinking, continuous improvement, and effective prioritization. These actionable tips provide a framework for making meaningful progress without compromising quality in pursuit of productivity.

Reflection on Case Studies and Personal Stories

Summary of Key Points

This chapter examined numerous case studies and personal stories that illustrate the importance of striking a balance between quality and quantity across various industries and personal pursuits. We examined successful organizations like Google, Toyota, and Patagonia, which have managed to strike this balance by fostering innovation, leveraging Lean principles, and committing sustainability. These companies demonstrated that prioritizing quality does not mean sacrificing growth or efficiency but enhances both.

On an individual level, we examined the stories of entrepreneurs, artists, and artisans who have achieved commercial success while maintaining their commitment to high-quality standards. Through continuous improvement, thoughtful decision-making, and a focus on long-term success, these individuals have found ways to avoid burnout and navigate consumer pressures, demonstrating that balance is achievable and essential for sustained success.

We also explored failures, such as the Volkswagen emissions scandal and the Boeing 737 Max crisis, offering lessons on what can go wrong when organizations prioritize quantity over quality. These stories served as cautionary tales about maintaining high ethical and safety standards, even in the face of market pressures.

Throughout the chapter, common themes emerged: the necessity of strong leadership, a clear vision, and a commitment to continuous improvement. These elements, along with an emphasis on adaptability and employee engagement, offer valuable insights for any organization or individual seeking to strike a balance between quality and quantity.

Encouragement for Application

As you reflect on these real-world examples and personal stories, consider how the lessons learned can be applied to your life or organization. Striving for a balance between quality and quantity is not an abstract ideal but a practical goal that can lead to long-term success, greater satisfaction, and meaningful impact. Whether you're leading a company, managing a team, or navigating your personal goals, the strategies outlined in this chapter—such as continuous improvement, effective leadership, and the pursuit of excellence—can help you find your middle way.

By applying these lessons, you can enhance your productivity while maintaining a high standard of quality, avoid burnout, and foster a culture of innovation and sustainability. Ultimately, striking this balance

Quality verses Quantity: Is There a Middle Way?

enables a more fulfilling and sustainable approach to personal and professional growth and success.

Embrace the opportunity to integrate these insights into your daily practices and long-term strategies, and you'll discover that quality and quantity can coexist, bringing lasting benefits to your life and work.

Quality verses Quantity: Is There a Middle Way?

Future Trends and Innovations

Technological Advancements: Artificial Intelligence and Machine Learning

In an increasingly data-driven world, artificial intelligence (AI) and machine learning (ML) transform how businesses make decisions. These technologies can process vast amounts of data at speeds and levels of complexity beyond human capacity. Through enhanced decision-making, automation, and improvements in customer service, AI and ML offer solutions that can balance quality and quantity in unprecedented ways.

Enhanced Decision-Making AI and ML can revolutionize decision-making processes by allowing businesses to analyze and interpret data more effectively. Traditional methods of analysis, though useful, are often limited in scope and speed. In contrast, AI algorithms can process and analyze complex datasets, identifying patterns and trends that might go unnoticed.

For example, AI applications are already used to predict consumer behavior. By analyzing purchasing history, social media activity, and weather patterns, AI models can predict what consumers are likely to buy, when they will make a purchase, and at what price point. This enables businesses to optimize inventory, minimize waste, and offer more personalized products or services. In supply chain management, AI helps optimize logistics by predicting demand and adjusting inventory levels to prevent overstocking or understocking. This ensures businesses maintain the right balance between efficiency and product availability, reducing costs without compromising quality.

Moreover, AI-driven tools are utilized in product quality control. These tools can detect defects or inconsistencies in manufacturing processes with a far higher accuracy than human inspectors, ensuring that the final product meets the highest quality standards without delaying production. By enabling more precise, data-driven decision-making, AI empowers businesses to balance quality and efficiency.

Automation and robotics are becoming increasingly integral to the manufacturing and retail industries. Automated systems allow businesses to produce more goods faster but without sacrificing quality. In fact, by reducing human error and fatigue, automation can enhance quality standards.

For example, robotics in manufacturing ensures that tasks are performed consistently and with precision. Whether it's assembling products or performing quality checks, robots can operate more efficiently and accurately than humans. This is especially important in industries where precision is critical, such as automotive manufacturing or electronics production. In retail, automated checkout systems and inventory management technologies enable businesses to track products in real-time, reducing the likelihood of errors and enhancing customer satisfaction.

In addition to improving efficiency, automation frees human workers to focus on more complex and creative tasks. This shift enables businesses to foster innovation while maintaining high operational efficiency. As industries continue to adopt automation, the challenge will be to ensure that quality standards are maintained and enhanced through these technological advancements.

AI in Customer Service: Customer service is another area where AI is making significant strides. With the rise of AI-driven chatbots and virtual assistants, businesses can offer 24/7 customer support. These tools can handle a wide range of customer inquiries, from basic questions to more complex troubleshooting. Moreover, AI allows these systems to learn from each interaction, gradually improving the quality of responses and offering more personalized experiences over time.

For example, AI-powered chatbots can analyze past customer interactions to tailor recommendations or responses. This creates a more seamless and satisfying customer experience. Unlike human agents, AI-driven systems can handle thousands of interactions simultaneously, ensuring customers don't have to wait long for assistance. This improves scalability without sacrificing the quality of service.

Furthermore, AI can help businesses gather and analyze customer feedback, enabling them to continually improve their products and services. By integrating AI into customer service processes, companies can maintain high engagement and satisfaction levels while optimizing their resources.

The rise of AI and machine learning represents an exciting opportunity for businesses to innovate and grow without compromising quality. By harnessing the power of these technologies, companies can enhance decision-making, streamline operations, and deliver high-quality products and services on a larger scale. Whether through predictive analytics, automation, or personalized customer service, AI is poised to play a pivotal role in shaping the future of quality management.

Internet of Things (IoT)

The Internet of Things (IoT) refers to a network of interconnected devices that can communicate with one another and collect, exchange, and act on data. As more industries adopt IoT, the potential for creating more intelligent, more efficient systems grows rapidly. This section will explore how IoT is applied in manufacturing and retail, two sectors where balancing quality and quantity is crucial.

Smart Manufacturing Smart manufacturing is revolutionizing the industrial sector by integrating IoT devices into production lines and facilities. These IoT-enabled systems enable manufacturers to monitor and optimize production processes in real-time, resulting in improved operational efficiency and enhanced quality control.

One of the key benefits of IoT in manufacturing is predictive maintenance. Traditionally, equipment failures could halt production, leading to costly downtime and product delivery delays. IoT sensors continuously monitor machines for performance, temperature, vibration, and other critical metrics. This data is analyzed in real-time, allowing businesses to predict when equipment might fail or require servicing. By addressing maintenance needs before a breakdown occurs, manufacturers can minimize downtime, reduce repair costs, and maintain consistent production schedules, all while ensuring that product quality is not compromised.

Additionally, IoT enables more effective resource management. Connected devices can track the consumption of raw materials, energy, and other resources, providing manufacturers with insights on optimizing their usage. For instance, IoT-enabled systems can automatically adjust production settings to reduce waste, minimize energy consumption, and align production rates with actual demand. This improves cost efficiency and helps maintain quality by preventing overproduction or resource shortages.

Furthermore, real-time monitoring of quality is a significant advantage. IoT sensors can detect defects or anomalies during production, enabling immediate corrective action to be taken. This precision ensures that only high-quality products reach the market, which is crucial for industries where quality directly impacts brand reputation and customer satisfaction.

In the retail sector, IoT is playing an increasingly important role in transforming back-end operations and enhancing the customer experience. From inventory management to improving in-store interactions, IoT is helping retailers strike a balance between efficiency and quality.

IoT devices are handy for inventory management. By using sensors and RFID (Radio Frequency Identification) tags, retailers can track products in real time, knowing exactly how much inventory is available at any given moment. This enables better stock management, as retailers can automatically reorder products when levels are low, avoiding overstocking and stockouts. Efficient inventory management ensures that customers always have access to the necessary products without unnecessary delays, improving operational efficiency and customer satisfaction.

Quality verses Quantity: Is There a Middle Way?

IoT is also improving supply chain optimization. Smart sensors track products from warehouses to retail shelves, ensuring inventory is moved quickly and efficiently. IoT-enabled tracking systems provide detailed insights into the location and condition of goods throughout the supply chain. For example, perishable items can be monitored for temperature and humidity during transport, ensuring they maintain their quality from the manufacturer to the store. By reducing delays and optimizing transport routes, retailers can ensure products arrive on time and in perfect condition, meeting customer expectations for speed and quality.

Beyond logistics, IoT enhances the in-store customer experience. Smart shelves equipped with IoT sensors can notify store employees when products need to be replenished or when pricing discrepancies are detected. Some retailers leverage IoT to offer personalized shopping experiences through smart mirrors, mobile apps, and beacons that provide tailored product recommendations based on customer preferences. These innovations enhance the convenience of shopping and improve the overall quality of the customer experience, ensuring that consumers feel valued and engaged.

Retailers like Amazon and Walmart are already utilizing IoT to streamline operations and enhance customer engagement. For example, Amazon's Go stores use IoT to enable cashier-less shopping, where customers can pick up items and walk out of the store with their purchases automatically charged to their accounts. This frictionless experience is a prime example of how IoT can enhance convenience without sacrificing quality.

IoT is enabling smarter, more efficient systems in both manufacturing and retail by providing real-time insights and control over processes. In manufacturing, it enhances predictive maintenance, resource management, and quality control, ensuring businesses can produce high-quality goods efficiently. IoT streamlines inventory and supply chain management in retail while improving customer experience, allowing retailers to deliver quality service at scale. As IoT evolves, its potential to help industries balance quality and quantity will grow stronger.

Quality verses Quantity: Is There a Middle Way?

Sustainable Practices: Circular Economy

The circular economy represents a shift away from the traditional linear model of production and consumption, which follows a "take, make, dispose" pattern. Instead, the circular economy focuses on closing the loop by designing products and materials out of waste, keeping them in use, and regenerating natural systems. As businesses and industries increasingly recognize the importance of sustainability, adopting circular practices is becoming a key strategy for enhancing long-term resilience and maintaining quality without depleting resources.

Principles of Circular Economy At its core, the circular economy aims to decouple economic growth from resource consumption, creating a system that is both restorative and regenerative by design. This model challenges the conventional "use and dispose" approach by emphasizing three key principles:

1. **Designing Out Waste and Pollution**
   In a circular economy, waste is viewed as a design flaw, rather than an inevitability. Businesses must reevaluate product design to ensure that materials can be reused, recycled, or safely returned to the environment. The goal is to eliminate waste and minimize pollution from the outset, creating products and processes that are more efficient and environmentally friendly. This approach often involves using fewer resources, selecting sustainable materials, and adopting clean manufacturing technologies that reduce emissions and energy consumption.

2. **Keeping Products and Materials in Use**
   The second principle focuses on extending the life cycle of products and materials by keeping them in circulation for as long as possible. This can be achieved through recycling, remanufacturing, and refurbishing strategies. Products are designed for durability, repairability, and reuse, ensuring they don't end up in landfills prematurely. For example, electronics companies may offer trade-in or repair programs, allowing consumers to return their old devices for refurbishment rather than disposal. Similarly, the fashion industry has embraced

clothing rental, resale, and repair practices to reduce textile waste.

3. **Regenerating Natural Systems**

   The circular economy aims to positively impact natural systems, rather than simply minimizing harm. This means utilizing renewable resources and enhancing ecosystems through sustainable practices. For instance, regenerative agriculture practices help rebuild soil health, improve biodiversity, and sequester carbon. By restoring and replenishing natural systems, businesses can ensure that their operations contribute to environmental resilience and long-term sustainability.

Adopting these principles offers businesses numerous benefits, including reduced resource costs and an enhanced brand reputation as socially and environmentally responsible entities. However, transitioning to a circular economy also presents challenges, particularly in redesigning existing systems and products to fit this model.

Case Studies: Circular Economy in Action. Many businesses have already begun adopting circular economic principles, experiencing the benefits and challenges firsthand. Below are examples of companies leading the way in this space.

1. **Patagonia**

   Patagonia, the outdoor apparel company, is a well-known advocate of sustainability and has long embraced circular economy principles. Through its "Worn Wear" program, the company encourages customers to trade in used Patagonia products in exchange for store credit. The returned items are then repaired and resold, keeping them in circulation rather than contributing to waste. Additionally, Patagonia focuses on designing durable, repairable products made from recycled materials, further aligning with circular principles. The company's commitment to sustainability has strengthened its brand loyalty and enhanced its reputation as a leader in ethical business practices.

One challenge Patagonia has faced is scaling these efforts while maintaining profitability. Repairing and reselling products is labor-intensive and costly, but the company views this as an essential part of its mission to reduce environmental impact.

2. **Renault**

    The French automobile manufacturer Renault is another example of a company that has successfully implemented circular economy strategies. Renault remanufactures used car parts, such as engines, gearboxes, and turbochargers, at its Choisy-le-Roi plant, thereby extending their life cycle. This process requires less energy and fewer raw materials compared to producing new parts, resulting in significant cost savings and environmental benefits. Renault also recycles materials from end-of-life vehicles, ensuring that valuable resources, including metals and plastics, are recovered and reused.

Renault's primary challenges are ensuring a consistent supply of used parts for remanufacturing and overcoming the perception that remanufactured products are inferior to new ones. However, through rigorous quality control and effective customer education, Renault has demonstrated that remanufactured parts meet the same standards as new components.

3. **Loop**

    Loop is an innovative startup that aims to eliminate single-use packaging by offering consumers durable, reusable containers for everyday products. Partnering with major brands like Unilever, Procter & Gamble, and Nestlé, Loop provides a platform where customers can purchase products in reusable containers that are collected, cleaned, and refilled. This system keeps packaging materials in use for multiple cycles, significantly reducing plastic waste.

Loop has faced challenges with the logistics of collecting and cleaning containers efficiently. The company addresses this by creating a streamlined consumer return process and investing in infrastructure to scale its operations. Despite these hurdles, Loop's model is gaining traction as consumers and corporations recognize the environmental benefits of reusable packaging.

The circular economy offers a pathway toward more sustainable business practices by focusing on designing out waste, keeping materials in use, and regenerating natural systems. Companies like Patagonia, Renault, and Loop have demonstrated the viability of these principles, though they face challenges in scaling and maintaining profitability. As more businesses adopt circular strategies, the balance between quality, sustainability, and economic growth will become increasingly achievable.

Green Technologies

The shift towards green technologies is driven by the need to address climate change, reduce operational costs, and ensure long-term sustainability. In this context, industries are increasingly adopting renewable energy sources and eco-friendly materials to minimize their environmental impact while maintaining or enhancing the quality of their products and services.

Renewable Energy: The adoption of renewable energy sources, such as solar and wind power, has seen significant growth in recent years across various industries. These energy sources are sustainable and can reduce operational costs over time. By investing in renewable energy, businesses can reduce their dependence on fossil fuels, lower greenhouse gas emissions, and contribute to global sustainability goals.

In terms of balancing quality and quantity, renewable energy provides businesses with a means to maintain or increase production capacity while minimizing environmental impact. For example, manufacturing facilities that integrate solar or wind energy can produce the same or greater quantities of goods while reducing their carbon footprint. Over time, the cost of renewable energy infrastructure, such as solar panels or wind turbines, is offset by savings on energy bills, allowing companies to remain competitive while upholding high-quality standards.

One notable example is Apple, which has committed to using 100% renewable energy across all its global facilities. By transitioning to renewable energy, Apple has reduced its environmental impact and set an industry benchmark for sustainability. This shift has been accompanied by a continuous focus on producing high-quality products, demonstrating that sustainability and quality coexist without compromising business goals.

The challenge for businesses, particularly those in heavy industries, is the initial cost of transitioning to renewable energy and maintaining a consistent energy supply. However, advancements in energy storage technologies, such as batteries, are helping to mitigate these concerns, making renewable energy a viable option for businesses that prioritize sustainability and quality.

Eco-Friendly Materials Developing and using eco-friendly materials in manufacturing and packaging represent another crucial aspect of green technologies. Companies are increasingly recognizing the need to reduce their environmental impact by transitioning away from traditional materials that are harmful to the environment, such as plastics derived from fossil fuels.

One area of innovation is in biodegradable plastics. These materials are designed to break down more easily than traditional plastics, reducing the long-term waste associated with packaging. For instance, companies are now producing packaging materials from plant-based sources, such as cornstarch or sugarcane, which decompose naturally without leaving harmful residues behind. This shift to biodegradable materials helps reduce the environmental burden of packaging waste without compromising the protective quality that packaging offers to products.

Another area of focus is the use of recycled materials. In industries such as construction and fashion, businesses are increasingly using recycled materials to create new products. For example, companies like Adidas have developed shoes made from recycled ocean plastics, while many clothing brands are embracing fabrics made from recycled cotton or polyester. These eco-friendly materials reduce the demand for virgin resources and offer consumers high-quality products that align with their values of sustainability.

Sustainable sourcing is another key trend, particularly in industries that rely on raw materials such as timber, cotton, and minerals. Companies that adopt sustainable sourcing practices ensure that their materials come from renewable sources and are harvested in a manner that does not deplete the environment. For example, IKEA has made significant strides in sourcing wood from responsibly managed forests. At the same time, brands like Stella McCartney champion ethical and sustainable fashion by using organic and recycled materials.

Businesses adopting eco-friendly materials often face challenges related to cost and scalability. Biodegradable and recycled materials can sometimes be more expensive than their traditional counterparts, and scaling their use to meet enormous production demands can be difficult. However, as consumer demand for sustainable products grows and green technologies advance, the cost gap is gradually closing.

Adopting renewable energy and eco-friendly materials offers businesses a path toward balancing quality and quantity through sustainable practices. Renewable energy helps reduce operational costs while supporting high production levels, and eco-friendly materials allow companies to maintain product quality while reducing their environmental impact. By embracing these green technologies, industries can move toward a more sustainable future where quality is not sacrificed in pursuing quantity.

Work and Lifestyle Innovations: Remote and Flexible Work

The COVID-19 pandemic dramatically accelerated the shift toward remote and flexible work arrangements, compelling businesses and employees to reassess traditional work models. What was once viewed as an alternative or temporary solution has become a permanent fixture in many industries, with companies adopting remote and hybrid work models to adapt to changing circumstances and employee preferences.

Impact on Quality and Productivity One of the most significant impacts of remote and flexible work has been the shift in how businesses approach productivity and employee well-being. While initial

Quality verses Quantity: Is There a Middle Way?

concerns focused on whether employees could maintain productivity outside the traditional office environment, studies have shown that remote work can, in many cases, enhance both productivity and the quality of work.

Remote work provides employees with greater autonomy over their schedules, enabling them to work during their most productive hours. This flexibility often leads to improved focus and fewer distractions compared to the office environment. Employees also report greater job satisfaction due to the increased work-life balance that remote work affords. The ability to structure work around personal responsibilities, such as childcare or household tasks, leads to less stress and burnout, contributing to higher-quality output over time.

However, remote work also presents challenges. Some employees struggle with feelings of isolation or a lack of direct communication with their colleagues, which can affect collaboration and creativity. In addition, without proper boundaries between work and personal life, employees may struggle to "switch off," leading to overwork and decreased long-term productivity. To balance quality and quantity, companies must establish clear guidelines and support systems to ensure remote workers remain engaged and connected while avoiding burnout.

The rise of flexible work arrangements, such as hybrid models where employees split their time between home and the office, offers a middle ground. Hybrid work allows employees to enjoy the benefits of remote work while still maintaining face-to-face interactions that foster team collaboration and company culture. Many businesses, including tech giants like Google and Microsoft, have adopted hybrid work models to provide employees with flexibility while ensuring the quality of collaboration and innovation.

Tools and Technologies The success of remote and flexible work hinges on using practical tools and technologies that enable seamless communication, collaboration, and project management. The rise of remote work has sparked a wave of innovation in software that helps teams stay connected, productive, and organized, even when working from different locations.

Quality verses Quantity: Is There a Middle Way?

Collaboration software, such as Slack and Microsoft Teams, has become essential for remote teams. These tools offer instant messaging, file sharing, and video conferencing capabilities all in one platform. They enable employees to communicate in real-time, share ideas, and collaborate on projects without being physically present. Video conferencing tools like Zoom and Google Meet have also become indispensable, facilitating virtual meetings and maintaining connections between team members.

Project management platforms, such as Asana, Trello, and Monday.com, play a crucial role in organizing tasks, setting deadlines, and tracking progress. These tools help remote teams manage workloads, allocate resources efficiently, and ensure that projects stay on track. With features like task assignments, timelines, and integrated communication, project management platforms enable teams to maintain productivity and deliver high-quality work, regardless of their location.

Several companies have successfully implemented these tools to transition to remote and flexible work models. For example, even before the pandemic, GitLab, a fully remote company, used a combination of Slack, Zoom, and GitLab's project management tools to facilitate collaboration across a globally distributed team. Automattic, the company behind WordPress, has also embraced remote work, using tools like P2 for asynchronous collaboration and Zoom for virtual meetings. These companies have demonstrated that remote teams can maintain high productivity and quality with the right tools while benefiting from the flexibility of working from anywhere.

Remote and flexible work arrangements offer businesses and employees a new way of working that prioritizes quality and productivity. Companies can ensure remote teams stay connected and productive by leveraging advanced collaboration software, project management platforms, and virtual meeting tools. As businesses adapt to the changing work landscape, the challenge will be finding the right balance between flexibility, productivity, and employee well-being.

Gig Economy and Freelancing

The gig economy has experienced rapid growth in recent years, fueled by technological advancements, shifting workforce expectations, and the increasing demand for flexible work arrangements. As more individuals turn to freelancing and gig-based jobs, the traditional workforce model is evolving, creating new opportunities and challenges for workers and businesses.

Rise of the Gig Economy The gig economy refers to a labor market characterized by short-term contracts, freelance work, and temporary positions, often facilitated by digital platforms. Gig work offers workers more control over their schedules and projects, unlike traditional full-time employment. This flexibility is one of the primary reasons people are drawn to the gig economy, as it allows them to manage personal commitments, pursue multiple income streams, and, in some cases, achieve a better work-life balance.

However, the gig economy also comes with trade-offs. While it provides workers greater flexibility, it often lacks traditional employment's job security, benefits, and stability. Gig workers often lack access to health insurance, retirement benefits, and paid time off, rendering them more susceptible to economic fluctuations and periods of low demand. This lack of security can stress gig workers, particularly when balancing multiple projects and clients.

The gig economy has transformed industries such as transportation (e.g., Uber, Lyft), food delivery (e.g., DoorDash, Grubhub), and creative services (e.g., Upwork, Fiverr), offering businesses flexible labor at a lower cost. While this model allows enterprises to scale their workforce up or down as needed, it raises questions about the long-term sustainability of relying on gig workers for essential tasks.

Balancing flexibility and job security in the gig economy remains a critical challenge. Some workers thrive in this environment, enjoying its freedom, while others struggle with uncertainty and a lack of support. Governments and businesses are now grappling with regulating the gig economy to provide better worker protection while maintaining the flexibility benefits that have made this model so popular.

Platforms and Opportunities The growth of gig economy platforms has made it easier for freelancers to find work, market their skills, and manage their projects. Digital platforms like Upwork, Fiverr, TaskRabbit, and Freelancer provide gig workers access to a global marketplace of clients seeking a wide range of services, from graphic design to writing to technical support.

These platforms offer freelancers the opportunity to take control of their careers by choosing the projects they want to work on, setting their rates, and building their brands. Many freelancers, particularly those highly skilled or able to niche into specific areas of expertise, have successfully navigated the gig economy to achieve financial independence and work-life balance.

For example, graphic designers, software developers, and digital marketers often use platforms like Upwork or Fiverr to secure long-term clients, allowing them to generate consistent income without the constraints of a traditional 9-to-5 job. These workers frequently cite the flexibility of working remotely and the ability to choose their projects as key factors in achieving a balanced, fulfilling career.

However, navigating the gig economy successfully requires specific skills beyond technical expertise. Freelancers must also be adept at self-marketing, time management, and financial planning, as they are responsible for sourcing their work, managing client relationships, and ensuring a steady stream of projects to maintain a consistent income. For many gig workers, building a solid reputation on these platforms and securing repeat business is crucial to achieving long-term stability.

One example of success in the gig economy is the story of freelancers transitioning from traditional employment to full-time freelancing during the COVID-19 pandemic. As businesses shifted online and demand for digital services increased, these freelancers leveraged their skills to build thriving careers by offering web design, content creation, or digital marketing services. By leveraging platforms like Upwork or

Fiverr, they can find clients worldwide, diversify their income streams, and create more balanced and flexible lives.

The rise of the gig economy presents a new model of work that prioritizes flexibility over traditional job security. Platforms like Upwork, Fiverr, and TaskRabbit have created new opportunities for freelancers to build successful careers. Still, gig workers must also navigate challenges related to income stability, benefits, and work-life balance. As the gig economy continues to grow, finding ways to support gig workers while maintaining the advantages of flexibility will be essential for ensuring a sustainable future for this evolving workforce model.

Educational Innovations: Personalized Learning

The field of education is undergoing a transformation, with technology playing a central role in personalizing the learning experience to cater to individual needs. Adaptive learning technologies and blended learning models are at the forefront of this shift, enabling more tailored and flexible educational experiences that strike a balance between quality and accessibility.

Adaptive Learning Technologies Adaptive learning technologies are designed to create personalized educational experiences by adjusting the content, pace, and difficulty level of learning materials based on individual student performance and preferences. Utilizing artificial intelligence (AI) and data analytics, these platforms assess how students interact with the material and adapt the curriculum in real-time, ensuring that each student receives a customized learning experience tailored to their strengths and weaknesses.

One of the most significant benefits of adaptive learning is its ability to meet the diverse needs of students. In traditional classroom settings, it can be challenging for educators to cater to each student's learning style and pace. Adaptive technologies bridge this gap by providing real-time feedback and modifying lessons based on students' progress. This personalized approach helps ensure that students who need more time on a particular subject receive the support they need, while those who grasp concepts quickly can move ahead without being held back.

Several platforms are already using AI to provide adaptive learning experiences. For example, platforms like DreamBox and Knewton offer personalized learning environments for subjects such as mathematics, where the system adjusts lessons based on students' performance. Another example is Duolingo, an AI-driven language learning app that adapts to the user's language proficiency, offering tailored exercises to improve specific skills. These platforms enhance learning outcomes, making education more engaging and accessible, and fostering a deeper understanding of the material.

The challenge with adaptive learning technologies is ensuring that they are effectively integrated into existing educational systems and that educators are equipped to use them. While these tools can enhance learning quality, they require support and training for teachers to maximize their impact.

Blended Learning Models: Blended learning models integrate online and offline educational environments, offering a flexible and personalized approach to learning. In a blended learning setting, students participate in a mix of traditional classroom instruction and digital learning activities, allowing them to benefit from the strengths of both environments.

Blended learning offers several advantages for both students and educators. For students, it provides greater control over their learning process. By incorporating online modules, students can learn at their own pace and revisit challenging material as needed, thereby fostering a sense of ownership over their education. This flexibility is particularly beneficial for students with diverse learning needs or those balancing other responsibilities, such as work or family commitments.

For educators, blended learning models provide the opportunity to enhance the classroom experience with digital tools. Teachers can utilize online platforms to track student progress, identify areas where students are struggling, and offer targeted support. Additionally, online tools enable more interactive and engaging learning experiences, such as simulations, videos, and games, which can make complex concepts more accessible.

One example of blended learning in practice is the flipped classroom model, where students are introduced to new content through online lessons before attending in-person classes for discussion, problem-solving, and application of the material. This approach shifts the traditional model of instruction, allowing students to absorb information independently and come to class prepared to engage more deeply with the content. The flexibility of blended learning models enables education to be tailored to individual student needs while maintaining high-quality standards.

Blended learning has been particularly effective in higher education and corporate training environments, where students or employees often require more flexible schedules. For instance, universities like MIT and Stanford offer blended learning programs that combine online lectures with in-person labs or group work. In corporate settings, companies utilize blended learning platforms to deliver online training modules while incorporating hands-on workshops for skill application.

Adaptive learning technologies and blended learning models represent the future of personalized education. By leveraging AI to tailor learning experiences and integrating online and offline environments, these innovations provide flexible, high-quality education that meets students' diverse needs. The challenge moving forward will be ensuring that these technologies are widely accessible and effectively implemented to provide the best outcomes for learners.

Lifelong Learning

In today's rapidly evolving world, lifelong learning is crucial for both personal and professional development. As industries transform due to technological advancements and global shifts, individuals must continually acquire new skills and knowledge to remain competitive and adaptable. Lifelong learning fosters continuous improvement, enabling individuals to meet the demands of an ever-changing job market while enhancing their personal growth and fulfillment.

The Importance of Continuous Education: The pace of change in the modern world has made continuous education crucial for staying relevant in various fields. With the rise of automation, artificial intelligence, and other disruptive technologies, many jobs now require skills that did not exist a decade ago. This reality has created a growing need for individuals to engage in ongoing education, not just at the start of their careers but throughout their lives.

Online courses, certifications, and professional development programs support this shift. Unlike traditional education systems, which typically focus on a finite learning period (such as a college degree), lifelong learning emphasizes the importance of regularly updating skills and knowledge to keep up with new trends and technologies. Professionals who commit to continuous education can position themselves for career advancement, stay competitive in the job market, and ensure their skills remain relevant as industries evolve.

For instance, industries such as IT, healthcare, and finance continually adopt new tools and practices, requiring workers to stay informed about the latest developments. Certifications in new software, methodologies, or regulations help professionals maintain a competitive edge and ensure their work meets current quality standards. Moreover, continuous education is not limited to technical skills; it also includes soft skills such as leadership, communication, and problem-solving, which are increasingly valued in today's work environments.

Beyond professional development, lifelong learning also enriches personal growth. It fosters curiosity, broadens perspectives, and encourages individuals to explore new interests, whether through academic subjects, hobbies, or creative pursuits. The growth mindset promoted by lifelong learning leads to a more adaptable and resilient individual capable of thriving in an unpredictable world.

Learning Platforms: The rise of online learning platforms has democratized access to education, making high-quality learning opportunities available to a much broader audience. Platforms like Coursera, edX, and Udemy have become household names in online education, offering a variety of courses, certifications, and degree programs across multiple disciplines.

Coursera is one of the most popular platforms. It partners with top universities and organizations, such as Stanford, Yale, and Google, to offer courses and certifications in subjects ranging from data science to the humanities. With flexible scheduling and a range of price points, Coursera makes high-quality education accessible to both professionals seeking to upskill and individuals looking for personal enrichment. The platform also offers fully accredited degrees, allowing students to earn a formal education without the traditional time and location constraints.

edX, co-founded by MIT and Harvard, offers courses from leading institutions worldwide. One of edX's strengths is its emphasis on high-quality, rigorous education miming traditional academic environments. With courses on cutting-edge topics such as artificial intelligence, sustainability, and digital marketing, edX enables individuals to stay ahead of industry trends while pursuing certifications that enhance their credentials. Moreover, edX has introduced MicroMasters and Professional Certificate programs that provide a stepping stone toward full degrees or specialized career paths.

Udemy is another major player, focusing on practical, skills-based learning. Unlike Coursera and edX, which are primarily partnered with universities, Udemy enables individual instructors to create and offer courses on a wide range of topics. This makes the platform highly diverse, catering to learners who want to develop specific skills, such as coding, graphic design, or digital marketing. Udemy's low-cost courses and user-friendly interface have made it particularly popular among freelancers, gig workers, and professionals looking to acquire new abilities quickly.

These platforms not only make education more accessible but also enable personalized learning experiences. Learners can choose their studies' pace, depth, and structure, fitting education around their personal and professional schedules. This flexibility promotes lifelong learning, allowing individuals to pursue continuous education without sacrificing other commitments. Furthermore, the interactive nature of these platforms—through discussion forums, peer feedback, and quizzes—creates a more engaging and dynamic learning environment than traditional self-study methods.

The importance of lifelong learning is more evident than ever as industries evolve and personal growth becomes a priority for many. Platforms like Coursera, edX, and Udemy are leading the way in providing accessible, high-quality education that can be tailored to individual needs. By embracing continuous education, individuals can maintain their professional relevance and personal development, ensuring a balance between the pursuit of quality and quantity in life and work.

Reflection on Future Trends and Innovations

The tension between quality and quantity has become more pronounced as industries and societies evolve. However, the future trends and innovations discussed in this chapter provide a blueprint for addressing this balance in ways that benefit individuals and businesses. By embracing technological advancements, sustainable practices, new work models, and lifelong learning, there is a clear opportunity to enhance efficiency and the quality of products, services, and personal achievements.

Summary of Key Points: The chapter explores how artificial intelligence (AI) and machine learning revolutionize decision-making, automation, and customer service. These technologies enable businesses to maintain high levels of quality while scaling operations and increasing output. For instance, AI-driven insights help optimize supply chains, while automation improves consistency in manufacturing processes without compromising quality. These technologies enable us to strike a balance between efficiency and excellence.

The **Internet of Things (IoT)** is enabling smart systems that allow industries such as manufacturing and retail to optimize their processes in real-time. With predictive maintenance and enhanced inventory management, businesses can reduce waste and improve resource utilization while maintaining high-quality standards. This trend exemplifies how technology can drive both operational efficiency and product quality.

The shift toward **green technologies**, such as renewable energy and eco-friendly materials, illustrates how sustainability can complement quality and quantity. By adopting renewable energy sources and sustainable materials, businesses can reduce costs, lower their environmental impact, and continue producing goods at scale, all while meeting customer expectations for high-quality products.

Regarding work and lifestyle innovations, remote and flexible work arrangements, supported by digital tools, enable individuals to strike a balance between productivity and well-being. These models would allow workers to focus on high-quality output without the traditional constraints of office environments, demonstrating that flexibility can enhance job satisfaction and efficiency.

The gig economy's growth demonstrates that flexibility does not have to come at the expense of productivity. While gig workers enjoy greater autonomy, platforms like Upwork and Fiverr help freelancers maintain a steady workflow, allowing them to deliver high-quality services at scale. This balance between flexibility and output underscores the gig economy's role in navigating the quality-quantity divide.

In education, **personalized learning** through adaptive technologies and blended models presents a vision of how quality education can be delivered to a broader audience without compromising its effectiveness. Similarly, the rise of **lifelong learning** and accessible online platforms empowers individuals to stay competitive and continuously improve their skills, ensuring that both personal growth and professional excellence can be achieved over the long term.

Encouragement for Adaptation and Growth As we look toward the future, it is clear that staying informed about emerging trends and innovations is not just an option—it is a necessity for both personal and professional success. The rapid pace of technological change and evolving societal expectations necessitate continuous adaptation and growth.

To succeed in this landscape, businesses and individuals alike must be proactive in adopting innovations that can enhance quality and efficiency. Whether leveraging AI to optimize processes, adopting sustainable practices, or embracing flexible work models, these trends offer tools for achieving a more balanced approach to quality and quantity.

Additionally, the importance of **continuous learning** cannot be overstated. In a world where skills and knowledge quickly become outdated, lifelong learning is essential for maintaining relevance and pursuing excellence. Platforms like Coursera, edX, and Udemy are making it easier to acquire new skills and stay at the forefront of industry developments.

The future holds immense potential for those who are willing to adapt. By embracing the innovations discussed in this chapter, individuals and businesses can achieve a harmonious balance between quality and quantity that fosters growth, sustainability, and long-term success.

Quality verses Quantity: Is There a Middle Way?

Reflecting on the Journey

As we conclude, we must reflect on our journey to explore the tension between quality and quantity. Throughout this book, we have examined how this dichotomy has shaped history, influenced industries, and impacted personal choices. The debate between quality and quantity is not new, but its significance has evolved in particularly relevant ways to our modern world.

Recap of Key Takeaways

The Historical Context: The roots of the quality versus quantity debate can be traced back to ancient philosophies and the early industrial revolution. Historically, the tension between producing more and producing better has been a central aspect of many societal developments. Ancient philosophers, such as Aristotle, contemplated the virtues of excellence. At the same time, the Industrial Revolution marked a turning point, where quantity—mass production and output became the driving force behind economic progress. Over time, this debate has shifted from early forms of craftsmanship, where quality was prized, to the rise of consumerism and mass production, where quantity took precedence.

However, as our understanding of sustainability and long-term value has deepened, we now see a return to focusing on quality in craftsmanship, innovation, sustainability, and customer experience. This shift suggests that while quantity has fueled rapid growth and expansion, pursuing quality remains vital in creating enduring success and fulfillment.

Balancing Acts in Various Fields Throughout this book, we have explored how different industries and aspects of life grapple with the need to balance quality and quantity:

- ➤ **In Business**, we analyzed how companies like Apple, Toyota, and Patagonia have scaled their operations while maintaining high-quality standards. These companies have demonstrated that through continuous improvement, quality management systems, and technological innovation, businesses can grow without compromising the integrity of their products.

- ➤ **In Personal Development**, we explored the strategies individuals can use to balance work and life, enhance productivity, and cultivate mindfulness. The philosophy of minimalism and the practice of intentional living highlighted how focusing on fewer, more meaningful pursuits can lead to a richer, more fulfilling life. This section emphasized that quality time, experiences, and relationships often outweigh the sheer quantity of tasks completed or material possessions acquired.

- ➤ **In Technology and Innovation**, the rise of AI, machine learning, IoT, and green technologies showed how advancements can help industries scale while maintaining or improving quality. We explored how these innovations can enhance decision-making, streamline production, and enable sustainable growth, proving that technology can be a powerful tool in balancing the need for efficiency with the imperative for excellence.

Each field illustrates that the balance between quality and quantity is not a binary choice but a spectrum that must be navigated with intention, strategy, and foresight.

Insights Gained

As we reflect on the diverse fields and industries examined in this book, several common strategies and principles have emerged that provide a roadmap for striking a balance between quality and quantity. These insights, drawn from both theory and practice, underscore the importance of continuous growth, innovation, and a customer-centric focus in achieving sustainable success.

Common Strategies and Principles One of the central themes throughout this book is the importance of **continuous improvement**.

Quality verses Quantity: Is There a Middle Way?

Whether in business, technology, or personal development, striving to enhance processes, products, and skills resonates strongly. Concepts like **Kaizen** in manufacturing, which emphasizes incremental improvements, and the focus on lifelong learning in education highlight the value of steady, deliberate progress. Continuous improvement enables a gradual increase in quantity without compromising quality, ensuring that growth is sustainable and aligned with long-term objectives.

Another key principle is the **customer-centric approach**. Across industries, businesses and individuals who prioritize the needs and experiences of their customers succeed in maintaining both high quality and efficiency. From Apple's meticulous design philosophy to Patagonia's commitment to sustainability, these examples show how placing the customer at the center of decision-making can guide companies toward achieving an optimal balance. Focusing on what truly adds value to the customer allows businesses to streamline operations without compromising quality.

Innovation also plays a critical role in striking this balance. Technological advancements, from AI-driven decision-making to renewable energy solutions, enable industries to produce more while maintaining high standards of quality. Innovation is not limited to technology, but also includes process innovations such as agile development and flexible work models. These approaches encourage businesses and individuals to adapt quickly, enabling them to achieve both scalability and excellence.

Real-World Examples Throughout this book, we've shared numerous **case studies** and **personal stories** demonstrating these strategies' practical application. Companies like **Toyota** have pioneered integrating quality into mass production through lean manufacturing principles, setting a benchmark for industries worldwide. Similarly, **Apple** has balanced product innovation and design excellence while expanding its global market reach, demonstrating how a commitment to quality can drive both sales and customer loyalty.

In **personal development**, the stories of individuals adopting minimalist lifestyles or embracing time-blocking strategies offer valuable lessons on how focusing on fewer, high-quality tasks or experiences can lead to greater personal fulfillment and productivity. The case studies in **sustainable practices** and the **circular economy** further illustrate how businesses, such as Patagonia and Renault, have successfully navigated the challenges of balancing growth with environmental responsibility, ensuring that quality in their operations is not sacrificed for scale.

These real-world examples and stories illustrate the practical applications of the concepts discussed in this book. They remind us that pursuing balance is not an abstract idea but a reality that businesses and individuals can achieve through intentional strategies and decisions.

The Importance of Balance

At the heart of the quality versus quantity debate lies the importance of finding balance. Balancing these two seemingly opposing forces is crucial for achieving long-term growth, fulfillment, and success, whether in personal life or within an organization. This balance ensures that individuals and organizations can thrive sustainably, making thoughtful choices that foster improvement without sacrificing well-being or integrity.

For individuals, achieving personal growth hinges on striking a balance between quality and quantity in various aspects of life. Whether managing work-life balance, pursuing meaningful relationships, or setting personal goals, focusing solely on quantity—whether in tasks, possessions, or achievements—can lead to burnout, stress, and dissatisfaction. Conversely, focusing only on quality can slow progress and create a fear of failure or lead to perfectionism.

Individuals must learn to prioritize what matters most to find the middle ground. This often involves making **mindful lifestyle choices** and understanding that more is not always better. Practices such as time-blocking or adopting minimalist principles help individuals focus on fewer but higher-quality activities, thereby fostering both personal satisfaction and productivity. For example, investing in meaningful relationships or focusing on fewer, yet more impactful, career goals can enhance overall well-being.

Moreover, **maintaining a work-life balance is essential for personal growth. Setting clear boundaries between work and personal time ensures that individuals can recharge and bring their best selves to both. This balance enhances productivity and mental and emotional well-being, facilitating** continuous personal development. By embracing a mindset of quality over quantity in personal pursuits, individuals can lead more fulfilling and purpose-driven lives.

For Organizations, the pursuit of balance between quality and quantity is equally vital for achieving **sustainable success**. Companies often feel pressured to increase output, grow market share, and scale rapidly in a competitive business environment. However, businesses that focus solely on quantity may see short-term gains but risk long-term damage to their reputation, customer loyalty, and employee satisfaction.

To thrive, organizations must strike a balance that aligns with their core values and long-term objectives. **Employee satisfaction** plays a significant role in achieving this. Companies that prioritize quality in their work environments—whether through offering flexible work models, fostering innovation, or encouraging professional development—see higher employee retention, engagement, and productivity. Employees who feel valued and supported are likelier to deliver high-quality work, driving the organization's success.

Customer loyalty is another key factor that hinges on quality. Companies that focus on delivering high-quality products and exceptional customer experiences create strong, lasting relationships with their customers. These organizations understand that while increasing sales and scaling operations are essential, consistent value delivery fosters long-term loyalty. By investing in quality management systems, innovation, and sustainable practices, organizations can scale responsibly while maintaining high standards.

Ultimately, the balance between quality and quantity leads to sustainable and fulfilling growth for both individuals and organizations. **It's not** about choosing one over the other but about thoughtfully recognizing when to prioritize quality and when to scale up production, output, or personal achievements.

Sustainable Success

Sustainable success for individuals and organizations hinges on finding the right balance between quality and quantity. This balance ensures long-term viability, resilience, and adaptability in an ever-evolving world. By focusing on both, individuals and businesses can grow and thrive, even in the face of rapid change.

Long-Term Viability Sustainable success requires focusing on the long term, where growth is steady and thoughtful. For individuals, long-term viability is rooted in **personal sustainability**—the ability to grow, learn, and evolve without sacrificing health, well-being, or fulfillment. This means making choices that balance quality, such as nurturing relationships and investing in self-care, with quantity, such as pursuing meaningful career and personal goals. Practices like lifelong learning, mindfulness, and work-life balance are essential for personal sustainability, ensuring individuals continue to grow without burning out.

For organizations, long-term viability comes from embracing **sustainable practices** that align with evolving societal values and consumer expectations. Businesses that adopt environmentally and socially responsible strategies—such as using renewable energy, sourcing sustainable materials, or implementing ethical labor standards—are better positioned to meet the demands of modern consumers and regulatory environments. Continuous improvement, employee development, and a commitment to quality help organizations grow sustainably, ensuring they maintain high standards of excellence as they scale. This careful balance between quality and quantity enables organizations to remain competitive and resilient.

Future Readiness: In today's rapidly changing world, future readiness is crucial for both individuals and organizations. Adapting to new trends, technologies, and market shifts requires agility and foresight, and those who successfully balance quality and quantity are best positioned to navigate these changes. Future readiness means preparing for the unknown and embracing opportunities for growth and improvement.

For individuals, future readiness involves staying informed about **emerging trends** and continually updating skills to remain competitive and adaptable. This mindset of lifelong learning enables individuals to strike a balance between the depth of expertise (quality) and the breadth of experience (quantity), ensuring they are well-prepared for both personal and professional opportunities. By continuously enhancing their knowledge and skills, individuals can confidently navigate career shifts, technological disruptions, and challenges.

For organizations, future readiness is about embracing innovation while remaining committed to their core values. Technologies such as artificial intelligence, automation, and machine learning provide businesses with the tools to scale operations and increase efficiency. Nevertheless, they must maintain high standards to foster trust and customer loyalty. Companies that invest in **technological advancements** and continuous improvement are better equipped to navigate disruptions and capitalize on emerging opportunities. Balancing innovation with the principles of quality ensures rapid and sustainable growth.

Sustainable success is achieved through the thoughtful balancing of quality and quantity. For individuals and organizations, this balance leads to long-term viability, enabling continuous growth, adaptability, and resilience in the face of future challenges. By embracing sustainability, innovation, and continuous improvement, we can ensure that success is attainable and lasting, aligned with both present and future demands.

Encouragement to Readers: Starting the Journey

As we reach the end of this exploration of quality versus quantity, it is essential to empower you, the reader, to embark on a journey toward achieving a more balanced and fulfilling approach to life, work, and growth. The balance between quality and quantity is not a one-size-fits-all solution but a dynamic process that individuals and organizations must navigate based on their unique circumstances and goals.

Practical Steps To help you get started, here are some valuable steps and actionable advice that can guide you in balancing quality and quantity in your personal or professional life:

1. **Set Clear Goals**: Begin by setting clear, achievable goals that reflect your desire for quality and your need to accomplish tasks efficiently. Whether in your career, personal life, or business, having a clear vision of success will help you maintain focus. Ensure that these goals align with your values and long-term aspirations.

2. **Prioritize Tasks**: Not all tasks are created equal, and learning to prioritize is essential for maintaining balance. Utilize tools like the Eisenhower Matrix to distinguish between urgent and crucial tasks, enabling you to concentrate on high-impact activities that align with your quality objectives. Eliminating or delegating less important tasks can free up time to focus on what truly matters.

3. **Embrace Continuous Improvement**: The journey toward balance is ongoing. Commit to continuous improvement in both your personal and professional life by regularly reviewing your progress, identifying areas for growth, and making adjustments as needed. Whether refining processes at work or making small lifestyle changes at home, minor incremental improvements can lead to significant long-term benefits.

4. **Manage Time Effectively**: Time management balances quality and quantity. Techniques like **time-blocking** or the **Pomodoro Technique** can help you allocate focused time for high-quality work while ensuring you meet deadlines and complete necessary tasks. By being intentional with your time, you can strike a balance between accomplishing more and maintaining high standards.

5. **Focus on Long-Term Gains**: Consider the long-term impact rather than just immediate results when making decisions.

Quality verses Quantity: Is There a Middle Way?

Whether investing in higher-quality tools or products, spending more time developing skills, or building deeper relationships, focusing on long-term value often results in better outcomes.

Personal Reflection As you embark on this journey, it's essential to regularly reflect on your progress and reassess your balance between quality and quantity. This self-reflection can be a powerful tool for growth, helping you identify areas of imbalance and opportunities for improvement.

1. **Keep a Journal**: Consider keeping a journal to track your journey toward balance. Reflect on what is working and where you are struggling. Writing down your thoughts, successes, and challenges will provide you with valuable insight into your personal growth and help you stay accountable to your goals.

2. **Schedule Self-Assessments**: Set aside time regularly—weekly or monthly—to assess how well you balance quality and quantity in different areas of your life. Ask yourself: Are there areas where I am prioritizing quantity over quality? Where might I need to focus more on efficiency or scaling? Regular self-assessments will ensure that you stay aligned with your goals and make necessary adjustments as circumstances change.

3. **Identify Areas for Improvement**: Reflect on your personal life and work environment. Are there areas where you can streamline processes without sacrificing quality? Can you delegate tasks that are consuming too much of your time? By identifying specific areas for improvement, you can take concrete steps toward achieving a more balanced approach.

The journey toward striking a balance between quality and quantity is ongoing and requires intention, reflection, and adaptability. By setting clear goals, prioritizing what matters most, and embracing continuous improvement, you can create a more balanced and fulfilling life, personally and professionally. Remember, this process is not about perfection but about making mindful choices that support sustainable growth and well-being.

Continuous Improvement

The journey toward balancing quality and quantity is not a one-time effort, but a continuous improvement process. Whether in personal development, professional growth, or organizational success, a commitment to improvement allows us to adapt, grow, and thrive in an ever-changing world. Individuals and organizations can find and maintain that delicate balance by embracing lifelong learning and dedicating themselves to self-improvement.

Commitment to Growth Continuous improvement requires dedication and adaptability. For individuals, this means regularly evaluating progress, seeking opportunities to learn new skills, and making incremental changes that lead to long-term benefits. It's about recognizing that growth is a journey, not a destination, and that each step forward—no matter how small—contributes to the larger goal of achieving balance and success.

An organization's commitment to improvement often manifests through practices like lean management and Kaizen, where small, ongoing changes are made to enhance efficiency, quality, and customer satisfaction. Companies that prioritize continuous improvement understand that adapting to new technologies, market trends, and customer needs is crucial for staying competitive while maintaining high standards.

Balancing quality and quantity is a dynamic process that requires regular reflection and action. As you move forward in your journey, commit to continuously evaluating where improvements can be made and remain open to change. Growth, both personal and organizational, depends on this ongoing effort.

Inspiring Quotes and Anecdotes To inspire your commitment to continuous improvement, here are some quotes and examples from individuals and organizations that have mastered the balance of quality and quantity:

1. **James Cash Penney**, founder of J.C. Penney, once said, "Growth is never by mere chance; it is the result of forces

working together." This quote reminds us that growth, whether in business or life, comes from a deliberate combination of effort, strategy, and continuous improvement.

2. The Japanese concept of **Kaizen**, meaning "change for the better," serves as a guiding principle for companies like Toyota, which has long prioritized incremental improvements in its production processes. By focusing on small, consistent changes, Toyota has scaled its production while maintaining its reputation for quality, illustrating how a commitment to improvement leads to long-term success.

3. **Steve Jobs**, co-founder of Apple, famously said, "Be a yardstick of quality. Some people aren't used to an environment where excellence is expected." This focus on quality and Apple's ability to produce products at scale demonstrate the power of maintaining high standards while achieving global success.

4. **Patagonia**, the outdoor apparel company, is a prime example of balancing sustainability with growth. Patagonia has earned customer loyalty and business success by committing to producing high-quality, durable products while maintaining environmentally responsible practices. Their approach demonstrates how continuous improvement can lead to both ethical and economic benefits.

Incorporating these ideas into your personal or professional life can be a powerful motivator for continuous growth. Whether through minor, consistent improvements or bold innovations, the pursuit of balance is achievable when driven by a mindset of ongoing improvement.

Final Thoughts: The Future of Quality and Quantity

As we look ahead, it is clear that the relationship between quality and quantity will continue to evolve, influenced by technological advancements and shifting societal values. The balance between these two forces is not static; it is a dynamic interplay that requires continuous reflection, adaptation, and action. In a world where technology is rapidly transforming industries and consumers and businesses are placing increasing importance on sustainability and ethics, balancing quality and quantity will remain at the forefront.

Evolving Landscape: Innovations that enable us to do more with less will shape the future of quality and quantity. **Artificial intelligence, automation, and data analytics** will allow organizations to scale production and services while maintaining, or even enhancing, quality. **Sustainability** will also play a larger role as businesses are increasingly called upon to adopt practices that reduce waste and minimize environmental impact. As societal values shift toward more conscious consumption, the demand for high-quality products and responsible production processes will grow.

In this evolving landscape, adaptability will be key. Those who remain informed about emerging trends, stay open to innovation, and continually seek improvement will be best positioned to succeed. It is not enough to choose between quality and quantity; the future demands that we integrate and balance both, using the tools and knowledge at our disposal to create lasting value.

A Call to Action As we conclude this journey through the intricacies of quality and quantity, I encourage you to apply the insights and strategies explored in this book to your life and work. Whether striving for personal growth, leading a business, or navigating new career opportunities, the balance between quality and quantity is achievable—and it is powerful.

By embracing continuous improvement, setting clear goals, prioritizing what truly matters, and staying adaptable in the face of change, you can create a life, career, or organization that thrives on excellence and efficiency. Pursuing balance is not about perfection but about making mindful choices that align with your values and lead to sustainable success.

Now is the time to take action. Reflect on the lessons you've learned, identify areas for improvement, and commit to making the changes

Quality verses Quantity: Is There a Middle Way?

necessary to achieve a balance that works for you. Remember, when quality and quantity are balanced, the potential for positive change and growth is limitless.

Quality verses Quantity: Is There a Middle Way?

Appendix

Glossary of Terms

Lean Principles

Kaizen: A philosophy centered around continuous, incremental improvement, emphasizing efficiency and waste reduction.

Jidoka: A Lean principle of automating processes while allowing humans to intervene when issues arise, ensuring quality control.

Kanban: A visual tool used to manage workflow by limiting work in progress and ensuring tasks move through the system efficiently.

5S: A workplace organization system for Sort, Set in Order, Shine, Standardize, and Sustain, focusing on creating a clean, organized, and efficient work environment.

Heijunka: Production leveling that smooths out demand fluctuations to improve efficiency and eliminate overproduction.

Andon: A system that provides immediate visual feedback about the status of processes, highlighting issues like defects or equipment failure.

Takt Time: The pace at which products or services must be completed to meet customer demand without overproduction or resource strain.

Gemba Walk: A Lean practice where leaders visit the place (Gemba) where work happens to observe, listen, and identify opportunities for process improvement.

Hoshin Kanri: A strategic planning method to align the organization's objectives with its day-to-day operations, ensuring consistent achievement of long-term goals.

Poka-Yoke: A technique used to prevent error processes, making it difficult for mistakes to occur or ensuring immediate detection of errors.

7 Wastes (Muda): The types of waste that Lean seeks to eliminate:

Overproduction: Producing more than necessary, often leading to wasted resources.

Waiting: Time lost due to delays between production steps.

Transportation: Unnecessary movement of materials or products.

Overprocessing: Performing more work than needed due to inefficient methods.

Inventory: Excess materials or products not being used.

Motion: Unnecessary movements by employees during the production process.

Defects: Errors that require rework or scrap, thereby reducing quality and efficiency.

Muri: Overburdening of equipment, employees, or systems, leading to breakdowns and inefficiencies.

Mura: Unevenness in production flow, causing delays, excess work, or underutilization of resources.

Quality Management

Six Sigma: A methodology aimed at improving processes by reducing variation and defects, focusing on achieving near-perfect quality.

TQM (Total Quality Management): A philosophy focused on embedding quality into every aspect of an organization, involving all employees in the pursuit of continuous improvement and customer satisfaction.

SPC (Statistical Process Control): A method for monitoring and controlling processes using statistical tools to ensure consistent, high-quality output.

QMS (Quality Management System): A system that documents processes, procedures, and responsibilities to achieve quality objectives and meet regulatory and customer requirements.

ISO 9001: A widely used international standard that specifies the requirements for a quality management system to ensure organizations meet customer and regulatory demands.

Process Capability: A measurement of a process's ability to consistently produce output that meets specifications.

Control Plan: A document outlining how process variables will be monitored and controlled to maintain product or service quality.

FMEA (Failure Mode and Effects Analysis): A structured approach to identifying and prioritizing potential failure points in a process, allowing for proactive solutions.

Risk Mitigation: Strategies to reduce the impact of potential risks in a project or process, ensuring quality and consistency.

Continuous Improvement

PDCA (Plan-Do-Check-Act): A cyclical method for continuous improvement involving planning a change, implementing it, checking results, and acting on those results to improve.

DMAIC (Define, Measure, Analyze, Improve, Control): A Six Sigma methodology for improving existing processes by defining problems, measuring performance, analyzing causes, implementing solutions, and controlling results to maintain improvements.

DMADV (Define, Measure, Analyze, Design, Verify): A Six Sigma methodology used to design new processes or products to meet customer needs and quality standards.

Root Cause Analysis (RCA): A method for identifying the underlying cause of a problem to prevent it from recurring.

5 Whys: A problem-solving technique that involves asking "why" multiple times (usually five) to drill down to the root cause of an issue.

Gemba Kaizen: The combination of Gemba (the workplace) and Kaizen (continuous improvement), focusing on improving processes directly at the source of work.

Operational Efficiency

Cycle Time: The total time it takes to complete one process cycle from start to finish.

Lead Time is the time between the initiation of a process and its completion, and it is crucial for measuring responsiveness and efficiency.

Throughput: The rate at which a system or process produces output, often a key metric in both Lean and Six Sigma for assessing process flow.

Bottleneck: A stage in a process that slows production due to limited capacity, negatively impacting overall efficiency.

OEE (Overall Equipment Effectiveness): A measure of how effectively equipment is used, including availability, performance, and quality.

Innovation and Creativity

Design Thinking: A user-centered problem-solving process often used to develop innovative products or services.

Innovation Funnel: A conceptual model representing how many ideas are generated, filtered, and refined to produce practical, innovative solutions.

Disruptive Innovation: A type of innovation that creates a new market or value network, disrupting and potentially displacing established market leaders.

Change Management

Resistance to Change: A natural reaction to changes in the workplace, which can hinder the implementation of new systems, including Lean or Six Sigma initiatives.

Change Control: A systematic approach to managing process changes, ensuring consistency, and minimizing disruptions in quality or operations.

Glossary of Acronyms

DMAIC – Define, Measure, Analyze, Improve, Control
The Six Sigma methodology enhances existing processes by identifying problems, measuring performance, analyzing root causes, implementing solutions, and controlling results to sustain improvements.

TQM – Total Quality Management
An organization-wide approach to continuously improving the quality of products and processes by fostering a culture of customer satisfaction and employee involvement.

SPC – Statistical Process Control
A method of monitoring and controlling a process using statistical tools to ensure it operates efficiently and consistently produces high-quality output.

PDCA – Plan, Do, Check, Act
An iterative four-step management method for continuously improving processes, products, or services.

QMS – Quality Management System
A formalized system that documents processes, procedures, and responsibilities for achieving quality objectives and meeting regulatory requirements.

ISO – International Organization for Standardization
A global organization that develops and publishes international standards, including quality management standards like ISO 9001.

FMEA – Failure Mode and Effects Analysis
A structured approach to identifying potential failure points in a process or product and prioritizing them based on their impact and likelihood of occurrence.

SIPOC – Suppliers, Inputs, Processes, Outputs, Customers
A tool outlines a process's key components, offering a high-level view to ensure all elements are considered during process improvement.

5S – Sort, Set in Order, Shine, Standardize, Sustain
A workplace organization method that improves efficiency and safety through cleanliness and order.

OEE – Overall Equipment Effectiveness
A metric used to assess the efficiency and productivity of equipment by considering availability, performance, and quality.

SMED – Single-Minute Exchange of Die
A Lean tool reduces the time required to transition from one process or product to another, thereby minimizing downtime and increasing flexibility.

KPI – Key Performance Indicator
A measurable value that indicates how effectively an individual or organization is achieving key business objectives.

Quality verses Quantity: Is There a Middle Way?

Additional Resources

Books

"The Lean Startup" by Eric Ries
A groundbreaking book that introduces Lean principles to entrepreneurship, focusing on validated learning, rapid experimentation, and iterative product development. Ries offers practical advice for building sustainable businesses by eliminating waste and focusing on what customers truly value.

"Lean Thinking" by James P. Womack and Daniel T. Jones
This foundational text on Lean principles explains the concepts of waste reduction, continuous improvement, and flow. Womack and Jones provide case studies of companies that have successfully implemented Lean thinking to improve productivity and quality.

"The Goal" by Eliyahu M. Goldratt
This business novel examines the Theory of Constraints, a methodology for identifying and mitigating bottlenecks in production processes. It's a compelling story that illustrates how quality and quantity can be balanced through systematic process improvement.

"Out of the Crisis" by W. Edwards Deming
Deming, one of the most influential figures in quality management, outlines his 14 Points for Management, which focus on achieving quality through leadership and a systematic approach to continuous improvement. This book is essential reading for understanding Total Quality Management (TQM).

"The Toyota Way" by Jeffrey Liker
This book offers an in-depth examination of Toyota's Lean production system, emphasizing continuous improvement (Kaizen), respect for people, and long-term thinking. It's an excellent resource for understanding how Lean principles can be applied to manufacturing and service industries.

"Six Sigma: The Breakthrough Management Strategy Revolutionizing the World's Top Corporations" by Mikel Harry and

Quality verses Quantity: Is There a Middle Way?

Richard Schroeder

This book introduces the Six Sigma methodology, which focuses on reducing defects, improving processes, and achieving near-perfect quality. The authors use real-world examples from companies like GE and Motorola to illustrate how Six Sigma can transform business performance.

"Atomic Habits" by James Clear

A personal development book that explores the power of small, incremental changes (micro-steps) in achieving continuous improvement. Clear's practical framework for building better habits aligns with the principles of Kaizen and Lean.

"The Power of Less" by Leo Babauta

Babauta explores minimalism in both personal and professional life, offering strategies for focusing on the essentials and eliminating excess. His approach is particularly relevant to discussions about striking a balance between quality and quantity.

"Gemba Kaizen: A Commonsense Approach to a Continuous Improvement Strategy" by Masaaki Imai

Imai's book is an excellent guide to Kaizen. It focuses on continuous improvement at the Gemba (workplace) and provides practical tools and examples for implementing Kaizen in manufacturing and service settings.

"Quality is Free" by Philip B. Crosby

Crosby's seminal work explains the concept of "zero defects" and the cost of poor quality. He argues that quality is not a cost but a way to improve profitability by preventing mistakes and focusing on getting things right the first time.

Articles

1. **"Competing on the Eight Dimensions of Quality" by David A. Garvin (Harvard Business Review)**
   In this article, Garvin outlines the eight quality dimensions: performance, features, reliability, and conformance. This framework enables organizations to understand what constitutes quality from a customer's perspective and to prioritize these elements effectively.

2. **"What is Lean?" by Michael Ballé (Lean Enterprise Institute)**
   This article concisely introduces the principles of Lean, emphasizing the elimination of waste and the pursuit of continuous improvement. Ballé uses examples from various industries to demonstrate the universal applicability of Lean thinking.

3. **"The Evolution of Lean Thinking" by James Womack (MIT Sloan Management Review)**
   Womack reviews the history of Lean thinking, from its origins at Toyota to its adoption across global industries. The article offers insights into how Lean has evolved and why it remains relevant in today's competitive business environment.

4. **"Continuous Improvement: The Key to Success" by Brad Power (Harvard Business Review)**
   Power highlights the importance of embedding continuous improvement into an organization's culture. He discusses how companies can build processes that support incremental improvements and maintain a focus on quality and efficiency.

5. **"Why Six Sigma is on the Rise" by Roger Hoerl (Quality Digest)**
   Hoerl explains why Six Sigma has become one of the most widely adopted quality management strategies. He details how the methodology helps organizations reduce defects and

Quality verses Quantity: Is There a Middle Way?

variability while improving customer satisfaction and profitability.

Websites and Online Resources

Educational Websites

Coursera (www.coursera.org)

Coursera offers online courses and certifications from top universities and organizations on Lean principles, Six Sigma, continuous improvement, and quality management. Courses are available for various skill levels, from beginner to advanced, allowing learners to apply these concepts in real-world settings.

Lean Enterprise Institute (www.lean.org)

The Lean Enterprise Institute is a leading resource for learning about Lean principles and practices. It provides educational materials, workshops, webinars, and access to a global community of Lean practitioners. The site offers case studies, books, and articles on how Lean principles can transform businesses across industries.

Project Management Institute (www.pmi.org)

The PMI is a trusted organization that provides project management resources. It includes extensive materials on Lean and continuous improvement. PMI offers certifications, such as Lean Six Sigma and Project Management Professional (PMP), as well as tools and templates for applying these methods in various project environments.

American Society for Quality (ASQ) (www.asq.org)

ASQ is one of the premier organizations for quality management professionals. The site offers certification programs in Six Sigma, quality engineering, and quality auditing, as well as providing access to a wealth of knowledge through articles, case studies, tools, and training, which helps businesses and individuals achieve higher quality standards.

Six Sigma Online (www.sixsigmaonline.org)

This website is dedicated to Six Sigma education and certification. It offers comprehensive training programs, ranging from Yellow Belt to Black Belt, and a library of free resources, including articles, blogs, and case studies on quality improvement and process optimization, all utilizing Six Sigma principles.

MIT OpenCourseWare (ocw.mit.edu)

MIT offers free courses on Lean manufacturing, supply chain management, and process improvement through its OpenCourseWare platform. This is a valuable resource for anyone looking to learn from one of the world's leading technical institutes at no cost.

Lean.org.uk (www.lean.org.uk)

The UK-based Lean Enterprise Academy offers resources, training, and support for implementing Lean principles in various industries. The website provides articles, case studies, and practical tools for continuous improvement, making it a valuable resource for Lean practitioners worldwide.

Gemba Academy (www.gembaacademy.com)

Gemba Academy provides online training in Lean and Six Sigma principles. Its subscription service grants access to a vast library of video tutorials, case studies, and webinars. It's ideal for individuals and companies looking to train their teams on continuous improvement methods.

GoLeanSixSigma (www.goleansixsigma.com)

GoLeanSixSigma offers training and certification in both Lean and Six Sigma methodologies. Their website is an excellent resource for practical tools, templates, and case studies, enabling users to apply Lean and Six Sigma concepts across various industries. They also provide helpful blogs, podcasts, and webinars on related topics.

The Kaizen Institute (www.kaizen.com)

The Kaizen Institute is a global leader in Lean and continuous improvement consulting. Their website offers workshops, training programs, articles, and resources that guide organizations in implementing Kaizen practices to achieve long-term sustainable improvements.

Udemy (www.udemy.com)

Udemy is an online learning platform that hosts numerous courses on quality management, Lean principles, Six Sigma, and continuous improvement strategies. Learners can find affordable, practical training tailored to various levels of expertise and industry needs.

Smartsheet (www.smartsheet.com)

Smartsheet offers many tools and templates for project management and process improvement. It is beneficial for implementing Lean and Six Sigma strategies, as well as providing templates for Kanban boards, PDCA cycles, and process flowcharts. The website also offers articles and resources on improving productivity and workflow management.

Project Management Tools

Trello (www.trello.com)

Trello is a highly visual project management tool that organizes tasks using boards, lists, and cards. It's ideal for managing projects using the Kanban methodology, allowing users to create customized workflows, track progress, and collaborate in real-time. Trello is simple yet powerful, making it a popular choice for individuals and teams working on continuous improvement initiatives.

Asana (www.asana.com)

Asana is a comprehensive project management platform designed to help teams organize work, track progress, and meet deadlines. It offers task assignments, timelines, project overviews, and reporting tools, making it easy to implement project management and continuous improvement strategies. Asana integrates with Slack and Google Drive, enhancing collaboration and productivity.

Quality verses Quantity: Is There a Middle Way?

Microsoft Project (www.microsoft.com)

Microsoft Project is a robust project planning and management tool that helps organizations plan, schedule, and track projects. It offers powerful features for resource management, task scheduling, budget tracking, and Gantt charts. Its versatility makes it a preferred tool for managing complex projects and ensuring continuous improvement through detailed planning and monitoring.

Monday.com (www.monday.com)

Monday.com is a flexible work operating system designed to manage projects, workflows, and processes. It provides visual dashboards, enabling teams to collaborate and track real-time progress. Monday.com is particularly useful for implementing continuous improvement strategies, offering customizable workflows, automation, and integrations with other tools to streamline project management.

Smartsheet (www.smartsheet.com)

Smartsheet combines spreadsheet functionality with advanced project management features. It helps teams manage work, automate tasks, and track performance. Its ability to create dashboards, Gantt charts, and project timelines makes it ideal for organizations implementing Lean and Six Sigma strategies, enabling real-time visibility into progress and potential areas for improvement.

ClickUp (www.clickup.com)

ClickUp is a comprehensive productivity platform that offers project management, time tracking, and collaboration tools. It provides task assignments, customizable views (list, board, calendar, and Gantt), and reporting dashboards. ClickUp's flexibility makes it suitable for individual and team use, helping users implement continuous improvement initiatives by visualizing workflows and progress.

Wrike (www.wrike.com)

Wrike is a collaborative work management platform designed for project planning, tracking, and collaboration. It offers real-time updates, task dependencies, workload management, and Gantt charts, making it an ideal tool for teams seeking to enhance productivity and manage continuous improvement projects. Wrike integrates seamlessly with various third-party tools, including Slack, Salesforce, and Microsoft Teams.

Notion (www.notion.so**)**
The notion is an all-in-one workspace that combines project management, note-taking, databases, and task management in one tool. It's flexible, allowing users to create customized workspaces to organize projects, track tasks, and collaborate. The notion is ideal for teams and individuals looking to apply Lean or Agile methodologies, with features that support visual workflows, such as Kanban boards and task prioritization.

Jira (www.atlassian.com/software/jira)
Jira is a powerful project management tool used primarily in Agile development environments, but it is also adaptable to various industries. It provides tools for tracking work, managing sprints, and monitoring continuous improvement efforts. Jira's customizable workflows, robust reporting capabilities, and seamless integration with other tools, such as Confluence, make it an excellent choice for managing both short-term and long-term projects.

Basecamp (www.basecamp.com**)**
Basecamp is a user-friendly project management tool that facilitates team collaboration and task management. It allows users to create to-do lists, assign tasks, set deadlines, and share files, making it ideal for continuous improvement projects. Its simplicity and focus on communication help teams stay organized without overwhelming them with complex features.

Quality verses Quantity: Is There a Middle Way?

Sources for Worksheets and Templates

For those looking to apply the strategies discussed in this book, the following websites offer a variety of worksheets and templates that can support your journey toward balancing quality and quantity, implementing Lean principles, and practicing continuous improvement.

Lean Enterprise Institute (www.lean.org)
It offers free templates and tools for lean problem-solving, PDCA worksheets, A3 reports, and value stream mapping. It's a great starting point for professionals looking to adopt Lean methods.

GoLeanSixSigma (www.goleansixsigma.com)
Provides downloadable templates, including DMAIC project charters, Fishbone Diagrams, 5 Whys worksheets, and SIPOC diagrams. Each template includes detailed instructions on how to use it effectively.

Smartsheet (www.smartsheet.com)
Features customizable project management and continuous improvement templates, including Gantt charts, Kanban boards, and workflow trackers, to support efficient project management and ongoing improvement. Smartsheet offers both free and paid versions, catering to a range of needs.

American Society for Quality (ASQ) (www.asq.org)
ASQ provides access to various quality tools, including control charts, root cause analysis forms, and FMEA worksheets. Non-members can access a selection of free templates, while members enjoy a broader range of resources.

Project Management Institute (PMI) (www.pmi.org)
PMI offers templates for various project management activities, including process improvement tools, risk management worksheets, and project charters, all of which are useful for Lean or Six Sigma projects.

Process Street (www.process.st)
Provides checklists and templates for business processes, including process audits, continuous improvement forms, and standard operating

Quality verses Quantity: Is There a Middle Way?

procedures. Their templates can be tailored to fit Lean or Agile methodologies.

Lucidchart (www.lucidchart.com)
A tool for creating process maps, flowcharts, and diagrams. Lucidchart offers templates for SIPOC diagrams, Value Stream Mapping, and other visual tools that support continuous improvement efforts.

Trello (www.trello.com/templates)
Offers pre-built templates for Kanban boards, task tracking, and workflow management. These templates are ideal for managing both personal tasks and professional projects.

Miro (www.miro.com)
A collaborative online whiteboard platform with templates for Kanban boards, process mapping, PDCA cycles, and more. Miro is particularly useful for teams working on Lean and Agile projects.

www.ingramcontent.com/pod-product-compliance
Lightning Source LLC
Chambersburg PA
CBHW052154220526
45471CB00004B/1671